Naturally, the only thing that could follow the enormously successful *The Art of Making Wine* was THE ART OF MAKING BEER.

Since the days of pubs and their delights in Egypt, Babylon and Rome, drinking beer has been almost a national pastime, though among the less educated in this fine art "beer" has become a generic name for ale, lager, and stout.

Making beer at home has graduated from a complicated art to one that can be done by almost anyone who buys this book and follows the explicit recipes. None of it is difficult and the production of one pint of beer — or of ale, stout, lager, or porter — costs about five cents. Simple instructions for making cider and perry are given also.

Beer to entertain your friends, to add enjoyment to your meals or to enjoy in front of your television set, is a part of gracious living and with all the refinements and all the varieties is available to you in the pages of this book.

By the same authors

The Art of Making Wine

The Art
of Making
BEER

**Stanley F. Anderson
with Raymond Hull**

HAWTHORN/DUTTON
New York

THE ART OF MAKING BEER

Library of Congress Catalog Card Number: 76-169864

ISBN: 0-8015-0380-9

13   14   15   16   17   18   19   20

CONTENTS

INTRODUCTION

There is practically no limit to the variety of beverages that can be, and are, successfully brewed at home. Yet in beverages, as in clothes, there are from time to time sweeping changes in what is regarded as fashionable and acceptable. In recent years there has been a definite trend towards the making and consuming of light-flavored beverages.

It has been said that no one really enjoys brandy till he is forty. That is because its potent flavor is best suited to the flagging gustatory sensibilities of older people. Young people have very sensitive taste buds, so to them old brandy and heavy red wines taste too strong. The changing fashion in home-brewing – like the changing fashions in automobiles, music and politics – is probably due to the increasing influence of youth on the thought and the consuming habits of our society.

Youth, as the saying goes, must be served, so this book tells how to make a number of beers and ales that are light in flavor and light in alcoholic content. I believe that these recipes will appeal to everyone who is young in years or young at heart.

Two other popular light beverages, cider and perry – made from the juice of apples and pears respectively – are by many drinkers considered as being comparable to beer; in some parts of the world they are sold and consumed side by side with beer. So I felt it was appropriate to describe them, too, in this volume.

And, for the sake of those who do prefer a drink with a bite to it, I have included some recipes that will tickle even the most time-worn taste buds.

There are some places where the home-brewing of beer is illegal. We do not advise anyone to violate the law. If you happen to live in such a place, and if this book comes into your hands, you must let your conscience be your guide.

The Art of Making Beer

1. Beer and Beermaking

"Come, my lad, and drink some beer."
— Samuel Johnson

We can easily imagine that the art of winemaking was discovered accidentally, when airborne yeast dropped into a bowl of grape juice and set it fermenting. It is harder to see how the fairly complex process of beermaking could have been found out by accident. Perhaps it was no accident at all, but the happy inspiration of some prehistoric genius.

Whatever its origins, beer has been brewed and drunk for at least six thousand years. It was known in ancient Egypt, in Babylon and China. The armies of imperial Rome drank beer, and carried all over Europe their knowledge of the brewing process.

Beer was welcomed particularly in the cooler countries of Northern Europe, where grapes could be ripened only with difficulty, or not at all. Barley, the basic ingredient of beer, is the easiest of cereals to grow. It matures in less than eighty days, and flourishes everywhere from the tropics to the Arctic Circle.

Moreover, wine needs, for good fermentation, a steady temperature above 60°F., but beer will ferment at 40°F. – a strong point in its favor with people of bygone times who lived in unheated houses in cool climates.

From Europe, especially from Germany, the art of beermaking was brought to North America. Most of the beer brewed and drunk on this continent is German-style lager.

1

Beermaking was at one time a domestic art; each household and each inn brewed its own. But as time went on, commercial breweries were established, making beer in large quantities and retailing it – in kegs and bottles – for home consumption, or by the glass through various kinds of public drinking establishments. As commercial breweries multiplied, home beermaking declined. Many people had neither the skill nor the patience to do it and, until Pasteur's work revealed the true nature of the fermentation process, home beermakers often had to put up with inferior beer or with complete failure of a brew.

But now home beermaking has been simplified. High-quality, tested ingredients are easily obtainable at specialty stores and, if you care to follow the simple instructions in this book, you can make good beer for yourself, your family and your friends, easily and economically – and, as a bonus, you will have some fun in the process.

TYPES OF BEER

"Beer", as the word is commonly used, is a generic term that includes a wide variety of beverages. But before naming the different kinds, let's look at the qualities they have in common.

They are all made by alcoholic fermentation, but much of their typical taste, color and aroma comes from the preliminary brewing process in which various ingredients are boiled in water before the addition of the yeast. (This is in contrast to winemaking, where most of the color and aroma are developed during or after fermentation.)

Beer, by comparison with wine, has a low alcoholic content, ranging from 3% to 8% alcohol by volume.

Most wines are "still" because all the carbon dioxide produced during fermentation is allowed to escape. But beer always contains more or less gas. Fermentation and bottling procedures are specially controlled to trap some of the carbon dioxide; kegs, bottles and cans are made strong to withstand the resultant pressure. When beer is served, the pressure is released and carbon dioxide boils out of solution and rises in bubbles to the surface.

2

"You were right, Martha – I bottled it too soon!"

Here again, beer differs from wine. In sparkling wines the bubbles rise and burst; in beer most of them do not burst, but collect at the top of the glass to form a layer of foam called the head. Connoisseurs like to see a thick, pure white, long-lasting head on their beer; so in beermaking we take various steps, to be described later, that give the beer good "heading quality."

The bubbling-off of trapped carbon dioxide is pleasing to ear and eye, but it has the additional advantage of heightening the stimulating effect of the drink. So, although a glass of beer contains only a small amount of alcohol, yet it gives you a noticeable lift.

Beer is a favorite drink with meals. Most beer drinkers agree that the tang of the hops sharpens the appetite and gives a clean, fresh taste in the mouth. Moreover alcohol, in small quantities, increases the flow of saliva and of the gastric juices essential to good digestion.

Now let's look at some of the better-known types of beer.

Lager

Lager is a light beer, yellow in color and translucent. It is fermented at 40°F. with a "bottom yeast" that settles to the bottom of the fermentor and needs little oxygen. Lager is highly charged with carbon dioxide and foams vigorously when poured. Its name comes from a German word meaning a store or warehouse, because it was originally made in the autumn, stored all winter, and consumed the following spring. It contains from 3% to 4% alcohol by volume and is best served fairly cold, about 40-45°F. It is lager that most North Americans think of when they mention beer.

Two famous European lagers are Pilsener and Dortmunder.

Vienna

Vienna beer is amber in color and has a mild, smooth flavor since it is brewed with less hops than most other beers.

4

Munich

Munich beer has a strong hop flavor and is dark brown in color. Its alcohol content varies, and may range up to 5% – noticeably stronger than lager.

Bock

Bock is a heavy beer, darker in color than lager, and with a stronger flavor.

Weiss

Weiss beer is made, not from barley, but from wheat malt. So it has a very pale color (*weiss* means white) and a distinctive, sharp flavor.

The above-mentioned beers contain less carbon dioxide than lager, and are usually served at about 45°F.

Ale

Ale is heavier and darker in color than beer. John Milton wrote of "spicy nut-brown ale." It is fermented with a "top yeast" that requires plenty of oxygen, and that tends to rise to the top of the fermentor. Ale yeast ferments well at temperatures up to 60°F.; so, if you have no place in your home cool enough for making lager, you can make ale instead.

The yeast, and the extra hops customarily added, give ale a stronger, more bitter flavor than lager. It contains more alcohol than lager – usually about 6% – and consequently requires extra aging in bottle if it is to develop its best strength and flavor. Indeed, a strong, dark ale, carefully prepared, will keep several years in the bottle, as long as most wines.

Porter

Charred or chemically colored malt gives porter its dark-brown color. It is a heavy, rich drink, with a sweetish, malty flavor resulting from the use of caramel, extra sugar, and only a little hops. It contains 4% to 6% alcohol.

Stout

Stout is a heavy, opaque, dark-brown drink. Some stouts contain licorice, which darkens the color to black and gives a characteristic flavor. The alcoholic content of stouts may be as high as 7% or 8%.

ALCOHOL CONTENT

We often have occasion to mention the alcohol content of commercial and home-brewed beers. On this subject there is considerable confusion of terminology, so a little clarification will be helpful.

In the U.S.A. the alcohol content of beer, when it is stated on the label, is expressed in percentage by weight; in Canada it is expressed in terms of British proof spirits. For example, a beer containing 3% alcohol by weight would be described as 3.4% alcohol by volume, and 5 degrees proof.

In this book we consistently express alcohol content in percentage by volume. For example, if we say an ale contains 5% alcohol by volume, we mean that 100 fluid ounces of the ale contain 5 fluid ounces of alcohol.

North American beer ranges from 3% to 6% alcohol by volume, and most of it is around 4%. When you brew your own beer, it would be easy enough to produce more alcohol, but it would be pointless. If you want the beverage to taste like beer, you have to keep its alcohol content down to the customary levels.

Moreover, the higher the alcohol content of the brew, the longer it takes to mature; so for quick results – and most home-brewers do want quick results – keep your beer down to the regular strength.

I suggest that you should gain experience by making several batches of 4% beer first; then you will have the skill and confidence to go on to the strong ales that call for a greater investment of time and materials.

COMMERCIAL BEERMAKING

Let's see how commercial brewers produce beer on a big scale; then we can consider how to adapt the process for use at home.

Malting

The first stage is to make malt. This is essential because before yeast can produce alcohol, the starch in the barley or other grain must be converted to sugar. Malt contains an enzyme, diastase, which effects this conversion. Here is the malting process:

1. The barley is cleaned and graded.
2. It is steeped in water for two or three days at a temperature of about 55°F. The grains absorb moisture, swell and become soft.
3. The soaked barley is allowed to germinate. It is stacked in heaps or put in big drums. To aid germination and prevent souring, the grain is aerated by periodically turning over the heaps, or by revolving the drums. Tiny shoots and roots grow from the grains. At this time the diastase is formed.
4. When the enzyme action has reached the right stage, germination is stopped by roasting the grain in a kiln. The kiln temperature determines the kind of malt that will be produced – 150-180°F. gives a light-colored malt, suitable for lager and other pale beers; higher roasting temperatures, up to 225°F., yield dark-colored malts for ale and stout. This kiln-drying lasts from 1 to 3 days.

Old-time brewers used to make their own malt. Now most of them buy it from specialized malt producers.

Brewing

The actual brewing process begins once the malt is made or bought.

1. The first stage is called mashing. The malt, mixed with water, is cooked for one to two hours in huge steam-heated tanks of copper or stainless steel. The temperature of the mash is precisely controlled, and is raised by steps, because different enzyme actions take place at different temperatures. For pale-colored beers, pressure-cooked cereals such as corn, rice or wheat may be added to the mash. The liquid finally drawn off from the mash tanks is called wort.

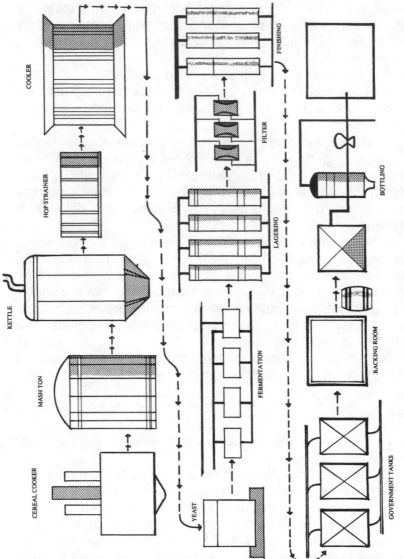

Brewery Flow Chrat

2. The wort is filtered and pumped into steam-heated copper brew kettles.

3. Hops are added, the quantity depending on the type of beer required, and the wort is boiled for 2-1/2 to 3 hours. This extracts the flavor from the hops and also sterilizes and concentrates the wort.

4. The hops, all their flavor spent, are strained out, and the wort is cooled, ready for "pitching" with yeast.

5. For lager, fermentation is conducted at 40-50°F. The yeast settles to the bottom and works rather slowly for 7 to 11 days. To make other beers a top yeast is used, at 50-60°F., and fermentation is over in 6 days or less.

6. The beer stands from 4 to 8 weeks in glass-lined clarification tanks. Yeast and other solid particles sink to the bottom. This process is speeded by chilling the beer to about 32°F. "Finings" may also be used, substances such as bentonite clay, gelatin, or isinglass which settle to the bottom and tend to carry with them the other suspended matter. The clear beer is carefully pumped out, leaving the sediment behind.

7. After clarification the beer is flat, and requires "finishing" to give it the desired sparkle. Carbon dioxide, extracted from the fermentation tanks, is injected under pressure and dissolves in the beer.

8. The finished beer is bottled, canned or put in kegs by special machinery that keeps it under pressure and so prevents it from foaming.

9. Cans and bottles are pasteurized at 140°F. for 20 minutes. This kills any remaining yeast cells and prevents any risk of renewed fermentation that might cause the containers to explode. Bulk beer in kegs is usually consumed within a few days of shipment and, even if not so consumed, will be kept under refrigeration, so it needs no pasteurizing.

This is the barest outline of what is in fact a very complex industrial process. There are many refinements that we have no space to describe fully. For example, brewers take great pains to select strains of yeast that will give the flavor they desire. When last I heard, there were 1400 different varieties of lager yeast alone, in addition to hundreds of varieties of ale yeast. Many brewers have to adjust the acidity or alkalinity of their water supply.

You may be sure that if there were an easier way to produce large quantities of good beer the commercial brewer would find and use it. But he takes great pains, and spends a lot of money, to ensure that his beer is consistent in flavor, color, effervescence and aroma. He has conducted extensive research to find out the tastes of his customers, and he must be sure of producing just what they want, *every time*. He cannot afford to throw out every tenth brew because it does not taste quite right.

Many breweries welcome visitors for conducted tours. Take such a tour if you can; you'll find it instructive. Specially noteworthy is the incessant striving for cleanliness of premises, equipment and personnel. Dust, dirt, air-borne yeasts and bacteria are the brewer's worst enemies, and he never lowers his guard against them. There's an important lesson here for the amateur.

AMATEUR METHODS

Although commercial beer is made very efficiently and is uniformly good, yet there are several sound reasons for making your own.

You save money by using your own labor and your own premises, and by avoiding the distribution and advertising costs, the retailer's markup, and the government taxes, which all form part of the price of commercial beer. So your homemade, first-quality beer costs you one-fifth to one-quarter the retail price of the equivalent commercial beer.

Another point is that all brewers in one district produce the same kind or kinds of beer. To be sure, many customers profess a fierce loyalty to this brand or that, but the preference is largely imaginary. Try the blindfold test with four or five locally produced beers and you will find how hard it is to pick your supposedly favorite brand.

This uniformity among all beers of one region caters to the presumed taste of the majority of beer drinkers there. But perhaps you are not one of the majority; perhaps the kind of beer

10

that is popular in your neighborhood does not please your palate; or perhaps, for variety's sake, you sometimes want to drink other kinds of beer. At some outlets, you have the choice of local beer or nothing at all; elsewhere you may be able to buy beer shipped in from distant breweries or from foreign countries at a considerably higher price than the local brew.

But when you brew your own beer, you can use all the basic recipes in this book. Those recipes alone give you a wider range of beers than you could find in many bars or liquor stores. Then, when you have gained some experience, you can begin to experiment, and produce a still greater variety of beers for the drinking pleasure of yourself, your family and your guests.

And of course we must not overlook the value of beer-making as a hobby. There's a keen satisfaction in conducting this age-old biological process in your own kitchen or basement. And, unlike some other hobbies, this one gives you a double pleasure – you have the interest of making the beer, and the satisfaction of drinking it.

No Malting

Malting barley, as you have seen from the previous description, is difficult and time-consuming, and in some places it is illegal for amateurs. So why bother, when you can buy good malt extract in varying grades and colors?

Brewing

I will describe, in general terms, the steps of the home-brewing process. Precise measurements, quantities and details for the various kinds of beer will be given in later chapters.

1. Prepare your yeast starter and assemble the other ingredients.

2. Make your mash. Boil the water (or as much of it as your boiler will hold) with the malt, brewing hops, and other ingredients, except sugar and yeast.

3. Pour the hot wort into your primary fermenting vessel, dissolve the sugar in it, cover it closely, and allow the hot mixture to cool.

11

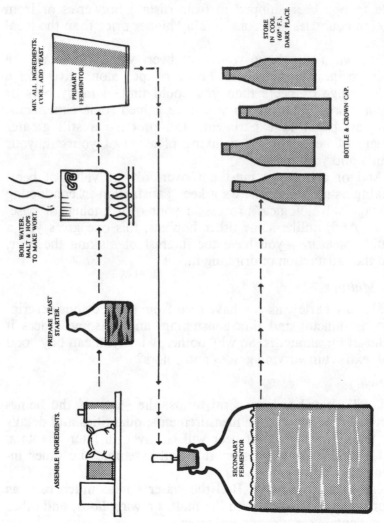

Home Flow Chart

ASSEMBLE INGREDIENTS.

PREPARE YEAST STARTER.

BOIL WATER, MALT & HOPS TO MAKE WORT.

MIX ALL INGREDIENTS; COOL; ADD YEAST.

PRIMARY FERMENTOR

SECONDARY FERMENTOR

BOTTLE & CROWN CAP.

STORE IN COOL (60° F), DARK PLACE.

4. Measure the specific gravity of the wort (see Chapter 4) and correct if necessary.

5. Add the yeast, cover, and ferment in a cool place.

6. Regularly measure the specific gravity of the brew to check the progress of the fermentation and consequent conversion of sugar to alcohol.

7. When the fermentation has slowed down, transfer the brew to your secondary fermentor, apply a fermentation lock to exclude air, and leave it until fermentation is complete and the beer is clear.

Some home-brewers skip the use of the secondary fermentor. They let fermentation work itself out in the stone crock or plastic tub and then bottle the beer at once. But there are several reasons why the use of a secondary fermentor is worth while:

a) By siphoning the beer into the secondary fermentor you get it off the heavy sediment that lies at the bottom of the primary fermentor. That sediment contains dead yeast cells, plus an assortment of vegetable matter. Left too long, it will begin to decay and impart unpleasant flavors to your beer.

b) Admittedly, a light sediment will be formed in the secondary fermentor, too. But that sediment is a layer of pure beer yeast, which you can reclaim and save as a starter for making fresh batches of beer. This economy soon pays the slight cost of carboy and fermentation lock.

c) The carboy has a narrow neck, so you can attach the fermentation lock and exclude air from the beer. This eliminates the risk of spoilage and of oxidation.

The more time I spend making beer myself, and dealing with the problems of beermakers, the more I am convinced that the most common problem of the amateur beermaker is oxidation. So the use of the secondary fermentor – or, for lagers, the completely anaerobic fermentation – is genuinely important.

If I had to choose between getting a primary or a secondary fermentor, I would use only the secondary, and conduct the entire process away from the air. This technique becomes increasingly feasible as we get better sources of hop extract.

You will notice that some of the recipes in this book call for the complete fermentation to be conducted in carboys.

So I strongly urge you to use the secondary fermentor. It pays for itself over and over again in better-tasting beer, reclaimed yeast, and elimination of spoilage losses.

8. Bottle the beer, adding a carefully measured quantity of sugar to start a renewed fermentation in the bottles that will yield the desired effervescence.

9. Age the beer in bottle in a cool, dark place.

10. Uncap, drink and enjoy the finished beer.

2. Equipment for Home-Brewing

The equipment for home beermaking is quite simple. Probably you already have some of the items in your kitchen. Such articles as you buy for this purpose will last you for years. Their cost per gallon of the beer they will produce for you is so trifling as not to be worth calculating.

I do not advise making beer 1 or 2 gallons at a batch. That is all very well for wine, a stronger beverage of which you may drink only three or four ounces at a time. But with beer, you will usually drink at least a 12-ounce bottle at a time, so 1 gallon would not last long with a family or with a party of guests.

I suggest that you begin by making 5 gallons at one brew, enough to yield about 55 bottles, yet not too much for one person to handle the processing with ease.

If, after some experience, you want to go on to make bigger batches, you will have little difficulty in enlarging the scale of your operations.

Here is a list of the equipment that I consider essential to making consistently good beer. I don't say it's impossible to make home brew – some of the time – with less equipment; but I do say that, with each item you reject from this list, your chances of failure will increase, and your standard of quality will drop.

BOILER

Unless you use one of the modern mixes with dry malt extract and hop flavoring, you will need a container for mashing, to boil up your water, malt and hops. It is highly desirable to boil all the water, so a boiler of 7 gallons is best, to give ample room for adding the malt, and for vigorous stirring. The boiler should have a lid.

You can use a stock pot or preserving pan of stainless steel, heavy enamelware (the enamel must be sound, without cracks or chips), or pyrex glass. Aluminum is not so good; some of the ingredients will react with it, and this may affect the flavor of the beer. Iron boilers are definitely not suitable.

If you cannot get such a large boiler, use the biggest one you have. The more of the mash you boil, the better will be the results. One gallon is the absolute minimum size.

PRIMARY FERMENTOR

Note that the primary fermentor must have plenty of spare capacity to give room for the foaming that occurs at this stage. If the vessel is filled nearly to the top, foam will spill over, and you risk contaminating your brew. So you need a wide-mouthed vessel of at least 1 gallon greater capacity than the batch you propose to ferment.

You can, in a pinch, use your boiler, but the handiest fermentor, I find, is a plastic tub; you can buy them at the hardware store, or at your home-brew supply house.

The so-called stone crock – actually glazed earthenware – makes a good primary fermentor. You can buy these crocks in various sizes at some kitchenware supply stores. You may be able to pick one up at a junk store, but be sure the glaze is perfectly sound. If liquid can get through the glaze, the porous earthenware beneath forms a fine breeding-ground for bacteria, and you have an incurable contamination problem on your hands. The stone crock has two disadvantages; it is heavy and it is breakable. Plastic vessels are light, and will stand up without damage to most accidental knocks.

A plastic trash-pail of 14 gallons capacity makes a good primary fermentor for a 10-gallon batch.

If you want to go on to big-scale production, you can get two kinds of large-capacity plastic containers. One is a heavy-duty plastic bag, about 6 to 8 mils thick, 6 feet long and 4 feet wide. This can be fitted inside any container that will support it, for example a steel drum or a wooden barrel. It costs only about a dollar, so is cheap enough to use once and throw away, if you want to avoid the trouble of cleaning it.

There are also semi-rigid plastic drum-liners, about 1/16 to 1/8 inch thick. They are stiff enough to stand on their own when filled with wort. They are easy to clean and, with moderate care, will last for years. They cost $20 to $25.

One word of caution: because of the complexity of the plastics industry and the wide variety of plastics used, you would be well advised to check new plastic containers for unpleasant odors. If any container has a very strong odor, I would suggest that you do not buy it, but use instead another manufacturer's product or, if you prefer it, glass.

But, if you take care to begin with suitable, odorless plastic vessels – and there are plenty of them on the market – you need not have the slightest fear that they will spoil the flavor of your beer. Countless thousands of home beermakers and winemakers use plastic fermentors, carboys and siphon hoses with perfect satisfaction. I use them myself, making beer for my own use. Commercial breweries use plastic hoses for moving beer from one vessel to another. In my opinion, people who complain about plastic vessels are using that as an excuse for bad flavors that really were caused by inferior ingredients or by careless processing.

COVER

Don't bother buying vessels fitted with lids. The best cover for primary fermentors of all sizes is a piece of sheet plastic, held down tight with string or elastic bands.

CHEESECLOTH

You have to boil the brewing hops with your mash, and then take out the spent hops. The best way to avoid the labor of skimming or straining is to use the principle of the tea bag. Get a yard of cheesecloth, put the hops into it, bunch the cloth over into a bag shape and tie up the neck. Then hang the bag, by a piece of clean string, in your mash boiler.

17

After you have removed the bag from the mash, untie the cloth and throw away the spent hops. Then wash the cloth, *thoroughly* rinse out the soap or detergent, dry the cloth and save it till next time.

NYLON STRAINERS

The modern nylon straining bags, now readily available, serve the same purpose as cheesecloth, and are so much more durable that they may be more economical in the long run. If you decide to use a nylon straining bag, buy a coarse one, so that you get a fairly rapid flow-through effect. After use, clean the nylon thoroughly, just as you would the cheesecloth.

STIRRER

You must do a good deal of stirring at various stages of the home-brewing process – to mix malt extract and water, to dissolve sugar, and so on. A wooden kitchen spoon is the handiest thing to use. Get a good big one while you are about it, so that you can quickly get 5 gallons of mash thoroughly stirred up.

If you have no spoon, a clean stick will serve the purpose, though rather less efficiently.

SIPHON

For transferring wort or beer from one vessel to another, far and away the easiest and safest technique is siphoning. Pouring is difficult or impossible – imagine trying to lift a 6-gallon stone crock, nearly full of wort, and pour from it into the neck of a carboy! Bailing with a saucepan, jug or some other dipper is easier; but you are bound to have some spilling and dripping, with accompanying risk of contamination. And anyway, you can't bail out of a carboy.

Siphoning is easy; it moves liquid without spillage or wastage and, what is most important, with the minimum exposure to air. Particularly for light lagers, air is the worst enemy. Every exposure to air by splashing, pouring or needless agitation darkens the color of the beer and impairs its flavor.

So, without any hesitation I recommend siphoning. For 5- and 6-gallon batches, 5 or 6 feet of rubber tubing, 1/4-inch internal diameter, will be plenty. You can use plastic tube if you like, but I find that the rubber is more flexible and easier to handle.

If you advance to big-scale production, 40 gallons or more at a time, you will need about 10 feet of plastic garden hose, 1/2-inch internal diameter. In this size, the plastic hose is easier to handle than rubber.

One warning: the siphon should be cleaned immediately after use, every time! It's easy to put the siphon tube down, intending to clean it later, and then forget. Then that tube, moist and dark inside, becomes a comfortable haven for spoilage bacteria that can ruin an entire batch of beer.

SECONDARY FERMENTOR

To contain your beer during the prolonged, quiet secondary fermentation, you need a container from which air can be excluded. For this purpose, nothing beats a carboy. You can buy glass carboys new or second-hand. Using a glass carboy, you can watch the fermentation in progress – many brewers enjoy the sight – and see how the beer is clearing. But glass is heavy and breakable, so many people are now using plastic carboys. Plastic is not heavy; it won't break; it is opaque and shields your beer from the light. (This is important. If you use a glass carboy, make sure it gets the very least possible exposure to light, including artificial light.)

At first, the most convenient size of carboy is one containing 5 gallons. You want to fill it nearly to the top, to keep oxidation to a minimum. For big-scale production you will find bigger carboys more convenient.

FERMENTATION LOCK

While your beer lies in the secondary fermentor, it is giving off carbon dioxide. You must let that gas escape, or the carboy will explode. Yet you want to prevent the entry of air, dust, wild yeasts and spoilage bacteria that would oxidize or otherwise contaminate your beer. So you close the fermentor with a one-way valve called a fermentation lock, set in a rubber bung that fits tightly into the neck of the carboy.

The fermentation lock contains a solution of potassium metabisulphite; the escaping carbon dioxide bubbles out through this solution, but air and contaminants cannot get in. A glance at the lock, to see how rapidly or slowly the bubbles are passing through it, gives you an easy way of estimating how near the fermentation process is to its conclusion.

Fermentation locks are made in several forms, of glass and plastic, and are sold quite cheaply in all home-brew supply stores. The glass models are rather fragile, so I recommend the plastic.

The metabisulphite slowly loses its sterilant potency, so you should refill the lock with fresh solution each time you make a new batch of beer.

THERMOMETER

Temperature control is essential to good beermaking. Wort that is too hot will kill your yeast; wort that is too cold will not ferment at all. Even within the temperature range where yeast ferments actively, an excess of a few degrees may noticeably impair the flavor of the finished beer, especially with the popular light lagers.

You will find that the most convenient thermometer is the immersion model that floats in the wort and gives an instant, accurate reading of its temperature. In a modern house, it will rarely be necessary to warm the primary or secondary fermentor. If you have to, tie an electric heating-pad to its side.

You are more likely to find that your brew is too warm. You can cool a primary fermentor by hanging in it a well-tied plastic bag of cracked ice. To cool a secondary fermentor, tie one or two plastic bags of ice on the outside, so that they lie on the shoulder of the carboy.

But these methods are only expedients. The best way is to find, or contrive, some corner in house, garage or storage shed where the air remains constantly at the temperature your brew needs for satisfactory processing. For example, a large closet in an unheated basement can be fitted with a small electric heater, controlled by its own thermostat, and – for fall and winter at least – your temperature-control problems are solved.

Then the temperature at which you store your finished beer largely determines the way in which the beer ages. So get an ordinary wall thermometer and hang it in the place where you keep your bottled beer.

Processing and storage temperatures for the various beers are given with the relevant recipes.

HYDROMETER

The hydrometer is an instrument that measures the specific gravity of liquids. It and its uses are fully described in Chapter 4.

FUNNEL

A funnel is useful for handling liquids, such as sugar syrup, that you use in brewing, and for pouring dry sugar into bottles, if you elect to use that bottling technique. A plastic funnel is best, with a neck small enough to go into the neck of the standard 12-ounce beer bottle.

GRAVY BASTER

An ordinary kitchen gravy baster – a rubber bulb mounted on a wide glass tube – is very handy for taking samples of wort or beer. Suppose your secondary fermentor is of opaque plastic; in a few seconds you can draw up a baster full of beer and see how well it is clearing. The baster is useful, too, for filling a hydrometer jar. In fact, you'll find many uses for it in your beermaking; it's one of the handiest accessories you can own. Of course, it needs scrupulous cleaning after use; otherwise it becomes a source of contamination.

SCALES

If you want to make good beer *every time,* you cannot dodge precise measurement of your ingredients. For 5

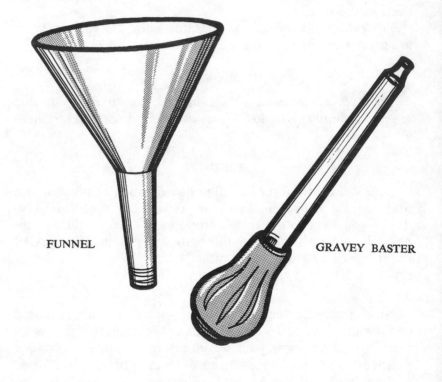

FUNNEL

GRAVEY BASTER

gallon batches, you will need a scale that weighs up to 5 pounds. For barrel-size batches, you should be able to weigh up to 50 pounds.

It is helpful if the scale (or another, smaller one) can weigh accurately to half an ounce, for ingredients such as hops that are used in small amounts.

Scales will generally pay for themselves, because they permit you to buy your ingredients in bulk, and therefore get a better price.

BOTTLES

The standard 12-ounce brown bottle is best for beer. It holds the right amount for one drink for one person, and the colored glass helps to exclude light, which is advantageous, especially with pale-colored beers.

If you prefer a larger container, you can use 30-ounce soft-drink bottles.

Warning: Never put beer in ordinary wine bottles, or any other bottle that is not specially designed to withstand internal pressure. Such bottles are likely to explode. At best you will lose your beer and have a nasty mess to clean up; at worst, you risk being disfigured or blinded.

Here is a labor-saving hint: rinse and drain your bottles immediately after you pour out the beer. It is much easier to get them clean then than if you wait until just before you are ready to bottle the next batch of beer.

CAPPING MACHINES

Corks are fine for wine, but for beer bottles you need crown caps that fit tightly over the bottle neck and resist the internal pressure. There are about half a dozen capping devices on the market. There is a simple little gadget that you hit with a hammer, and that sells for around $3; more complicated models from France and Italy range up to $30 or $40. I would suggest that you examine the various cappers available in your area, and settle for one that will last, and that will make a sound, tight closure every time. It is most irritating to save $2 on a capper which then causes you to lose five dozen bottles of beer!

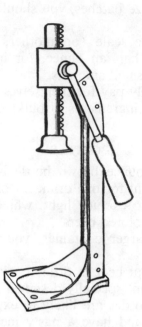

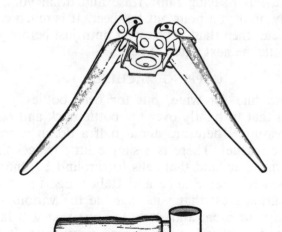

Capping Machines

The key to successful beermaking is cleanliness. It is not enough that bottles, fermentors, siphons and other equipment should be free from visible dirt. They should be biologically clean, free from any micro-organisms that might spoil the brew.

For all such cleaning of bottles and equipment, before and after brewing operations, chlorinated detergent from your home-brew supply store is very good. Chlorine kills all spoilage organisms, but it also kills beer yeast, so be sure that this detergent is thoroughly rinsed away before you put wort into the clean vessels.

Do not use household chlorine bleach. It is not the same thing as the chlorinated detergent.

Quaternary ammonium compounds are very powerful bactericides, although they are not cleansers. They are sold in highly concentrated form, and usually need dilution to two parts per thousand in warm water. Carefully follow the directions that come with these compounds, for use and for the subsequent rinsing of equipment.

An excellent bottle cleaner is a compound known as TSP. This, too, should be well rinsed away before you put the beer into the bottle.

You don't need to use these sterilants in large quantities. To sterilize a primary fermentor, for example, or a carboy, pour in half a pint of the solution; tilt the container so that the solution washes over every part of the interior. Drain out the solution, rinse with clean water, and your fermentor is ready for use.

(Of course, it's no use cleaning a vessel like this and then leaving it open to the air for hours or days. The best way is to sterilize a fermentor just before you fill it with mash or wort.)

Note: Potassium and sodium metabisulphite, so commonly used as sterilants in winemaking, are not recommended for beermaking, except in fermentation locks. If the least trace of metabisulphite gets into beer, it almost invariably reacts to produce hydrogen sulphide, the gas with the loathsome rotten-egg odor. For filling fermentation locks, make a solution of one Campden tablet in 4 ounces of water or, for larger quantities, 2 ounces of metabisulphite in 128 ounces water. Keep this solution in a tightly stoppered bottle.

All this equipment need not cost much more than twenty dollars. If you shop around second-hand stores and ask among your friends, you can assemble it for considerably less. It will serve for making all kinds of beers, and for cider and perry. If you want to turn your hand to winemaking, the same equipment will be useful again.

3. Ingredients

Your fermented beverages can be no better than the ingredients they are made of. That doesn't necessarily mean that you have to buy costly ingredients; the wrong ones are no cheaper than the right ones. So let us see, in this chapter, how to get best value for money, by using those ingredients that will give good-tasting, good-looking beer, cider and perry.

YEAST

The function of yeast in brewing was, for many centuries, quite unknown. Brewers used to skim the foam off one batch of fermenting beer and use it to start the next batch, without knowing what it contained and why it worked (or, sometimes, did not work). Then in the mid-19th century Louis Pasteur conducted his researches into the fermentation process and revealed the nature and function of yeast.

Yeast is not, as some people think, an inorganic chemical like common salt; neither is it a vegetable substance like hops, to be added to a brew, so many ounces to a batch, to produce a desired flavor.

Yeast is a microscopic, egg-shaped living organism which, under favorable conditions, grows and reproduces itself by division. Examine a drop of fermenting wort under a microscope; you will see yeast cells putting out buds which break

Scale Dia 2¼ = 500x

Saccharomyces ellipsoideus

Scale Dia 2⅜ = 800x

Acetobacter

off from the parent cell and then grow, bud and divide independently.

There are countless varieties of wild yeast flying and lying about everywhere, in the street, in your garden, in your house, on the fruits and vegetables you bring home from the supermarket. Some of these wild yeasts, to be sure, do convert sugar to alcohol. But many of them make the conversion inefficiently, using a lot of sugar to produce a little alcohol; some of them make, not only alcohol, but various unpleasant tasting byproducts as well.

The most dangerous contaminant is the vinegar bacteria, acetobacter, which consumes alcohol and turns it into vinegar. Once a brew becomes infected by acetobacter, you may as well throw it out, because there is no way to reverse the alcohol-to-vinegar transformation.

The ever present risk of contamination by acetobacter is one of the reasons why we take such pains to clean and sterilize equipment, and to keep air away from fermenting wort and finished beer. We must also exclude insects such as fruitflies, which commonly carry wild yeasts, acetobacter, and other contaminants on their feet.

So, by proper precautions, we keep a clear field for the operation of a selected, domesticated variety of yeast that will use the sugar efficiently, produce alcohol quickly, and leave us with a beverage that tastes good.

To grow, beer yeast must be not too warm and not too cold; it must have water, some form of fermentable sugar, and certain vitamins and minerals. In these conditions, the yeast converts sugar to alcohol and carbon dioxide gas – roughly equal parts by weight of each. We try to save all the alcohol; that is what gives beer its light stimulating effect. We let most of the carbon dioxide escape, but keep back a part of it in solution, to produce the characteristic effervescence of the finished beer.

The yeast also produces minute quantities of other substances that help to give the beer its flavor and aroma. Moreover, the type of yeast you use affects the clarity and heading quality of your beer.

So it is fair to say that yeast is the most important of your ingredients, and that your treatment of the yeast will largely determine the success or failure of your brew.

Admittedly, baker's yeast from the grocery store will make an alcoholic liquid that looks something like beer, but that liquid will be vastly inferior to the beer produced by a proper beer yeast.

Yeast and Temperature

Yeast placed in a suitable nutrient solution goes through two stages, growth and fermentation. In the growth stage, the sugar and other nutrients are used to make more yeast, and very little alcohol is produced. But when the concentration of yeast reaches a certain level, it stops increasing.

The time that elapses between addition of the yeast and the end of the growth stage is called the "lag period". During the lag period there is more risk than at any other time that the wort will be contaminated by undesirable wild yeasts, moulds or other organisms that would multiply there and spoil the brew.

After the lag period, the fermentation stage begins. The wort bubbles and hisses vigorously; sugar and nutrients are rapidly transformed into alcohol and carbon dioxide. At this stage, when the wort is heavily laden with active fermenting yeast cells, it is less susceptible to contamination.

For best results, the two stages need different temperatures. For the growth stage – for increasing the quantity of yeast – the temperature should be about 70°F.

Below this temperature, growth is slower, above it, faster. But there are risks in trying for very rapid growth. Temperatures above 75°F. may weaken some yeasts and reduce their ability to produce alcohol. Above 85°F. any yeast will be weakened, and at 95°F. most are quickly killed.

Some published recipes advise adding yeast when wort is at blood heat, 98.6°F. This is simply asking for failure!

For safe, certain and reasonably rapid growth of beer yeasts, I recommend a temperature of 70°F.

Now for the fermentation stage. Beer yeast works at a much lower temperature than do wine yeasts. Lager yeast will produce alcohol at 40°F., and most commercial brewers ferment lager between 40° and 50°F. Ale yeast enjoys a little more heat. Good fermenting temperatures for ale range up to 60°F.

To sum up this point, you need one temperature for growth of yeast, and a lower temperature for fermentation. The safest and easiest method is to grow a large, vigorous culture of yeast – we call it the "starter" – at 70°F. *before* you make your wort. Then add yeast to wort and ferment at a suitable lower temperature. We shall discuss these techniques in detail later on.

Buying Yeast

Beer yeast is generally sold as a liquid in a vial, or dry in a package. In my view, the best beer yeast cultures now available in the world are in the liquid form; they keep in good condition for eight to twelve months – even longer if refrigerated at 40°F. But such great advances are being made in processing the dry yeasts that, by the time this reaches print, some of the many brands of dry yeast may be as good as the liquids. Certainly the dry yeasts are easier to use.

If you buy a liquid yeast, *always* make a yeast starter. I prefer to make a starter even when using such large quantities as 5 or 10 grams of dried beer yeast. This ensures that you have a really large volume of active yeast to "pitch" or inoculate your wort.

Yeast Starters

We have seen that the lag period is the most risky part of the brewing process. There sits that crock of appetizing sugar, malt, vitamins and minerals, not yet fully occupied by your yeast, a veritable banquet for hungry microbes.

If, to 5 gallons of wort, you added the yeast culture as you bought it in liquid form, you would probably have a lag period of a week or more, and a correspondingly high risk of contamination by the spoilage bacteria that are floating everywhere in the air. To minimize the risk, you want to make the lag period as short as possible. The way to do that is to make a yeast starter, a large, vigorously multiplying culture of yeast – at least 3% of the total volume of your wort – that will spread through the wort and get the growth stage over as soon as possible.

Beer yeast is often sold with instructions for its use but, to be on the safe side, I will go over the process here. It is not complicated or time-consuming, and the preparation of the starter is worth every bit of the slight labor it involves. In fact, it is the key to sure-fire, high-quality beermaking.

To make a starter for a batch of 5 gallons, you will need the following equipment:

> 1 clean, sterile bottle, capacity 64 ounces
> Fermentation lock to fit the bottle

Here is the procedure. Take:

(a) *either*	(b) *or*
4 cups water	4 cups water
2 tbsp malt extract	4 tbsp Wine-Art Yeast Starter
1 pinch Vita Vin	pure beer yeast
pure beer yeast	

1. Sterilize the bottle. Bring the water to the boil in an enamel or stainless steel pan. Add the malt or yeast starter and boil for 3 minutes. If you are using method (a) add the Vita Vin. Take the pot off the stove.

2. Warm the sterile bottle under the hot-water tap, pour in the hot mixture and temporarily plug the bottle-neck with a piece of cotton wool.

3. When the mixture has cooled to about 70°F. add the yeast culture, then apply the fermentation lock.

4. Keep the bottle in a dark place at a temperature about 70°F.

5. Don't expect to see the spectacular growth that would occur in a similar culture of bread yeast. But between 24 and 48 hours from the start you should see very fine bubbles rising from the bottom. Now when you gently shake the culture it will throw up a white foam similar to the head on a glass of beer. When you see this, the starter is ready, and it should be used while it is in this active condition.

FERMENTATION LOCK

RING OF FOAM

BUBBLES RISING

SEDIMENT

Yeast Starter

You can, if you wish, keep a starter alive for some time in the crisper section of your refrigerator, at a temperature around 40°F. With lager yeast, feed it once a month. Take it out and gently pour off the clear liquid, leaving the deposit of yeast at the bottom. Then pour in a *cool*, sterile solution of malt and water, like the solution you started with. For ale yeast, it would be better to feed it twice a month.

Saving Yeast

There is no need to buy new yeast every time you want to make beer; you can carry over yeast from one brew to the next. As soon as you have siphoned the clear beer out of your secondary fermentor, put a funnel into a clean, sterile beer bottle. Swirl the sediment around in the carboy, then pour it into the funnel. You will have at least a quarter of a bottle of solid beer yeast; you may find that you have much more – even enough to fill part of a second bottle. Cap the bottle at once, and keep it in the crisper section of the refrigerator. The next time you make beer you can use this yeast and save yourself the trouble of preparing a new starter. Do not take the bottle from the refrigerator until you are ready to use it, and uncap it as soon as you take it out, because there will be some pressure in the bottle and, if it gets too warm, it may explode.

You can save lager yeast in this way up to three weeks, and ale yeast up to ten days. The reason you cannot keep the yeast too long like this is that while it is stored it is autolyzing, that is, feeding on itself, so in time it is completely consumed.

While there's no need to buy new yeast every time, it is worth noting that the breweries do not subculture their yeast more than five times before going back to the master culture for a fresh yeast. Amateurs are not likely to be more successful than the commercial brewers in maintaining purity.

Caution

This caution applies to all phases of handling and storing yeast. Remember that the air is laden with spoilage bacteria and wild yeasts which, from your point of view, are vastly inferior to your pure beer yeast. So, if you keep exposing a yeast starter or culture by taking off the cover to smell it, or to show it to your friends, it will sooner or later get contaminated. Take every precaution to keep your starters, or your stored yeast, pure and uncontaminated; you are thus taking the most important step towards getting sure-fire, consistent results from your brewing.

Don't Skimp

Some people, I find, are scared of their yeast. They think that, if they use too much, it will make the beer taste unpleasantly "yeasty". There is no basis for this fear. As a general rule for amateurs, I would say, "You can use too little yeast – you cannot use too much."

I have recommended using as a starter at least 3% of the total volume of the brew. You will do very well to make 4% or 5% instead. The bigger and more vigorous the starter, the shorter the lag period, and the smaller the risk of contamination.

The so-called yeasty taste comes from one or both of the following causes:

a) You have used the wrong kind of yeast.

b) You are drinking the beer too new, before it is properly aged.

The remedies are obvious.

Yeast for Cider and Perry

Beer yeast would be quite unsuitable for making cider and perry. You need a yeast specially bred for winemaking. The easiest way is to use a good all-purpose wine yeast such as Andovin, which comes in foil envelopes, each containing enough for making 5 gallons of cider or perry. With this ready-to-use yeast you are not compelled to prepare a starter; simply open the envelope and pour the yeast into the primary fermentor. This method is particularly convenient for those busy people who can give only one afternoon or one evening a week to their winemaking. Nevertheless the advantages of using a good, big starter are so out-

35

standing that I do recommend making a starter, even with Andovin. Andovin ferments well at 55° to 65°F., but is weakened by temperatures over 75°F.

Some people like to use champagne yeast for cider and perry. If you want to try that, get a pure champagne yeast culture and make a starter 3 days in advance. For 5 gallons, use a 32-ounce bottle and make a solution of "yeast starter", obtainable from any wine supply store. This solution contains all the necessary nutrients to produce a quick, vigorous growth of your yeast culture. Have the solution about 60° to 70° F., add the yeast culture and plug the neck of the bottle with cotton wool. In a day or two you will see bubbles rising through the solution, and the starter is then ready for use.

HOPS

Many amateur brewers, I find, take great pains and spare no expense to buy what they think is the best malt for their purpose. Yet some of them give little thought to choosing their hops. The hop, *humulus lupulus,* is a perennial climbing vine, a member of the mulberry family. The part we use for brewing is the female seed-cone, collected and dried in the fall of the year. Hops grow wild in many parts of the world, but between wild hops and good brewing hops is as big a difference as that between the wild crabapple and fine orchard apples. Many selected varieties of hops are cultivated in North America – Cluster, Kent, Brambling, Brewer's Gold, to name a few.

Hops give beer the clean, bitter flavor without which it could hardly be called beer at all. Beer with hops keeps longer than it would without them. (Remember that, with its low alcohol content, beer does not have the self-preservative qualities of a wine that contains 12% or more alcohol by volume.) Hops help your beer to hold an attractive-looking head of foam when it is poured, and they provide an important ingredient of the typical beer aroma.

So if you are really interested in making good beer, choose your hops with care. Stale hops are not good enough; a package that has been lying around unsealed for months on the

Hops

shelf of a grocery store will not be fresh, and will not give you good beer. Buy the freshest hops you can find. They should be green, and very aromatic.

Commercial brewers take great pains to keep their hops fresh, storing them under controlled conditions of temperature and humidity. They spend a lot of money on buying the best hops. If they cannot make good beer without good hops, neither can you.

So take a little extra trouble, and spend a few extra cents, to get good hops, and you will be repaid many times over by a great improvement in the quality of your beer.

BARLEY

Barley seems to add body to ale, and definitely affects the flavor. Some people like the barley flavor, others don't. On this point you can experiment and decide for yourself. Where a recipe calls for barley, you have the choice of Light Malted Barley, Crystal Malted Barley or ground Patent Black Malted Barley, all now readily available and much superior to raw barley.

MALT

As I pointed out earlier, you will not have to bother with making or using malt. Malt extract is easily available, and just as good. It comes in several grades and colors, from extra pale for lagers or pale ales, right up to heavy black for stout. It is primarily the malt that controls the color of the finished brew.

Malt extract is usually sold in cans containing 2-1/2 lbs.

SUGAR

Some commercial breweries use no sugar. The alcohol in their beer is derived solely from malt, such as barley malt, rice malt, and various cereal grits. This is the old, traditional method. But because of the current demand for very pale lagers, many breweries now use sugars of the type called monosaccharides.

There's no need to go deeply into the chemistry of sugar. It's sufficient to say that ordinary cane sugar from the grocery store is what is called a disaccharide. Yeast cannot act directly on a disaccharide. Admittedly, I recommend using ordinary cane sugar for cider and perry, but that is because apple and pear juice contain enough acid to invert cane sugar and turn it into a monosaccharide which is easily dealt with by the yeast. (Or if the juice is deficient in acid, we add it.)

What happens if you do use cane sugar for beer? The yeast will produce an enzyme called invertase that eventually inverts the sugar and allows fermentation to proceed. But for various reasons this process leaves a slightly sour after-taste that cannot be eliminated from the beer. This sourness is one of the most common faults in home-brewed beer.

Some home brewers who make English-style bitter ales feel that they can get away with using cane sugar, and that the strong flavor of the finished ale will mask the sour taste from the disaccharide. My own practice – and I recommend it to you – is to use monosaccharides for all your beermaking, even for the heaviest ales.

The best and cheapest monosaccharide is dextrose from corn, commonly called corn sugar. You can buy it at specialty shops in bags from 4 lbs. to 100 lbs. The approximate price is 18 cents to 20 cents a pound.

I do not recommend corn syrup — although this contains dextrose – because it usually has some extra flavoring such as vanilla, and not everybody enjoys beer that tastes like ice cream!

WATER

In making beer, and especially in a delicate-flavored pale lager, the water you begin with can markedly affect the final taste. Even though it is all supposed to be pure and palatable, tap water varies greatly from place to place in its content of dissolved minerals and gases, and in its flavor. Here are some hints for getting the best possible results, whatever your water supply may be like.

a) *Chlorination.* Heavy treatment with chlorine, so common in this era of widespread water pollution, is ruinous to the flavor of beer. Fortunately, boiling the water drives off the chlorine. (It also thoroughly sterilizes the water, killing any micro-organisms that have survived the chlorination.)

With water containing less than 5 parts per million of chlorine, some home-brewers feel they can get by without boiling. Nevertheless, I think it is a good idea to boil all the water for your beer if you possibly can.

b) *Hard water*. Boiling also tends to settle or separate some of the excessive mineral content of hard water.

c) *Soft water*. Soft water is excellent for making lagers, but for ales many commercial and home brewers prefer hard water. The ale recipes in this book call for the addition of water treatment, which contains calcium sulphate, to harden the water slightly. However, if you know that your local water is quite hard, omit that item from the recipe.

d) *Water analysis*. Some home-brewers blame the local water for the poor quality of their finished beer. If you take the precautions described above, you should have no trouble on that score. But if you are sure that you are doing everything else right, and the beer still does not taste as it should, you can have a sample of your water analyzed by your public health authority, or by some nearby university.

HEADING AGENTS

Some home-brewed, and even some commercial beers, have a poor head of foam. Others, that do form a nice head when the beer is poured, cannot hold it for long.

Although the head is mostly for appearance, I think it is quite important. The head should be pure white, about 1/2 inch to 3/4 inch thick, and it should hold at least 20 minutes after the beer is poured.

If the beer is fermented cool – that is, under 65°F. – with sufficient fresh hops, it will usually produce a thick, long-lasting head. But I personally think it is worth while to use some form of additive to ensure a good head.

A quarter to 1/3 stick of licorice added to the basic 5 gallon batch of wort will help the heading quality. Use the hard medicinal licorice sold in drugstores. Freeze it in the ice-making compartment of your refrigerator. When it is hard-frozen you can powder it with a kitchen food-grater, or wrap

40

it in a cotton cloth and pulverize it with a hammer or mallet. Then stir it into the boiling wort.

Licorice certainly helps to make a good head, but it does have some disadvantages. It naturally tends to darken the brew somewhat, so it won't be suitable if you want to make very pale beers. Also it tends to soften the beer a little – to take out some of the bite of the hops. Some people enjoy the softer flavor, others don't. You must decide for yourself.

If you do not want to use licorice, but still want to be sure of a good head, you can buy commercially made heading liquid from your home-brew supply house. It is not expensive, and it will definitely help the heading of the brew without changing its color or flavor.

Add the heading agent just before you bottle, then be careful to handle the beer gently, because otherwise the heading agent will produce excessive foaming during the bottling process.

CAMPDEN TABLETS

A Campden tablet contains about 7 grains of potassium metabisulphite. Dissolved in a slightly acid solution such as apple or pear juice, it releases approximately 4 grains of sulphur dioxide (SO_2). One tablet dissolved in 1 gallon gives 60 parts per million of SO_2.

At this concentration, few people can taste or smell the SO_2, yet it is an effective sterilizing agent. It inhibits the growth of the wild yeasts and spoilage organisms that lie on the raw fruit and float in the air, but it does not destroy cultured wine yeasts. So it gives you a completely controlled fermentation.

Moreover, Campden tablets slightly increase the acidity of the juice which, in most cases, is beneficial.

Always crush Campden tablets before mixing with a liquid.

ANTIOXIDANT TABLETS OR CRYSTALS

Pure ascorbic acid added to cider or perry at the time of bottling helps to prevent oxidation. One tablet – 100 milligrams of ascorbic acid – is enough for 1 gallon.

If you are working with large volumes of cider or perry, ascorbic acid crystals are more economical. Use 1 teaspoon for 5 gallons.

Sodium erythorbate is another excellent antioxidant. You can purchase it at your home-brew supply store.

ENZYMES

In Chapter 6 I mention that pectic enzyme breaks down the pectin in fruit pulp and releases more juice, more tannin, more flavor. Considerable research is being done upon enzymes. One new enzyme, rohament "p", already available in Europe, may soon be on the market here.

A recent convention of European brewers discussed a new enzyme that has largely eliminated the use of malt in beer-making. The brewer need use only 15% malt; the other 85% can be raw barley, plus this enzyme – a great economy. At the time of writing, this enzyme is not sold to amateurs, but it may be before long.

Watch for news of these and other new enzyme products; they can help you save money, and produce better fermented beverages.

Enzymes must always be used at an early stage of processing; their beneficial effect is exerted on the solids, and once those have been removed, there is little that enzymes can do.

4. Sugar Control

To make any fermented beverage, we set yeast to work converting sugar into alcohol. The proportion of alcohol in the finished beverage determines to a large degree its flavor, its stimulating effect, and its keeping quality. And that quantity of alcohol obviously depends on the quantity of sugar in the wort, apple juice or pear juice that you begin with.

It is not easy to measure that sugar by weighing. To be sure, you weigh the corn sugar that you use for a batch of beer. But how much sugar is there in the malt extract? How much sugar does your yeast starter contain after it has been fermenting for two or three days? How much sugar will be derived from the cereals such as barley that you add for some beer recipes? And, for cider and perry, how much sugar is there in the juice from any particular batch of apples or pears?

More questions arise at other stages of the fermentation process. What is the best time to transfer the partly finished brew from the primary to the secondary fermentor? When is beer ready for bottling? In bottling, have you added just the right amount of sugar that will give a brisk fermentation in the bottle, but not so much as to cause uncontrollable foaming, or to burst some of the bottles?

You can answer all these questions, and you can make good beer, cider or perry *every time,* by the easy process of sugar control. Let's see how this is achieved.

SPECIFIC GRAVITY

One pint of sugar solution weighs more than one pint of pure water; one pint of alcohol weighs less than a pint of water. Sugar solution is *denser* than water; alcohol is *less dense* than water.

The ratio between the density of a liquid and the density of water is called the *specific gravity* of that liquid.

Suppose Liquid A has exactly the same density as water; we say that its specific gravity is 1.000. (Specific gravity is usually measured to three decimal places.)

If Liquid B is denser than water, its specific gravity (usually abbreviated to S.G.) is greater than 1.000.

Let's take a practical example. When you begin to make a light lager your wort, containing sugar, malt and various other ingredients, will be considerably denser than water. Its S.G. will be about 1.030. As fermentation progresses, sugar will be converted to carbon dioxide gas, which escapes, and to alcohol, which is lighter than water. So the brew becomes less and less dense and, when fermentation ends, its S.G. will be about 1.000.

So if you can measure the S.G. of the wort, you have a good indication of how the fermentation is proceeding. Fortunately there is a cheap, simple instrument, the hydrometer, that will give you quick, accurate readings of specific gravity.

THE HYDROMETER

The hydrometer looks something like a thermometer with a swollen lower end. It is weighted so that it floats upright in a liquid. Inside the hydrometer tube is a graduated scale. To read the instrument, you see where the surface of the liquid cuts the scale; that reading gives you the S.G. of the liquid.

The denser the liquid, the higher the hydrometer floats, just as a ship rides higher in salt than in fresh water; so the *high* S.G. readings (meaning that the liquid is denser than water) are at the *bottom* of the scale, and *low* S.G. readings are at the top.

Because it is so often used for measuring the sugar content of liquids, this instrument is referred to by some brewers and in some books as a saccharometer. But in this book I shall stick to the term hydrometer.

HYDROMETER SCALES

There are many different models of hydrometer, designed for different scientific and industrial purposes. Consequently there are six or seven different methods of graduating them. The two most popular in English-speaking countries are the S.G. scale already mentioned and the Balling (or Brix) scale, which directly indicates the percentage by weight of dissolved solids – for our purposes mainly sugar, but including non-fermentable proteins in malt, or acids in apple and pear juice.

One popular type of Balling hydrometer scale reads from 0 to 30. Zero means that there is no sugar present; it is equivalent to 1.000 S.G., or pure water. A Balling reading of 30 means that 30% by weight of the liquid is soluble solids.

Most English winemaking and brewing literature uses the S.G. scale; the Balling scale is more popular in America. A complete conversion table for the two scales is given at the back of this book, so that with an S.G. instrument you can quickly calculate sugar content, and with a Balling hydrometer you can calculate specific gravity. Thus you can use recipes from any source.

Even more convenient are the hydrometers now available that contain S.G. and Balling scales side by side.

In home-brewers' conversation, and in print, the graduations of the hydrometer scale are often called degrees. For example, you may read, "when the S.G. of the wort drops 20 degrees, siphon it into the secondary fermentor." Similarly, Balling scale divisions are often called degrees.

There's no objection to this terminology, so long as you don't confuse hydrometer degrees with the thermometer degrees that are so important in home brewing.

There is one other thing that could lead to misunderstanding. You will often hear and read S.G. measurements given in abbreviated form, quoting only the digits that follow the decimal point. For example, S.G. 1.115 would be given as 115; 1.030 would be given as 30; 0.995 would become 995.

It's important to remember that because of the omitted unit figure and decimal point, a reading of 30 is *higher* than one of 995. In this book, for the sake of clarity, I shall print S.G. readings in full.

Different brands of hydrometers have different ranges, some of them needlessly wide. A range of 0.990 to 1.170 will be ample for the making of beer, cider and perry; it will also serve for any winemaking you may undertake.

USING THE HYDROMETER

You cannot very well take accurate hydrometer readings by dropping the instrument into your primary or secondary fermentor. Often a layer of foam hides the surface of the liquid. Moreover the sides of the vessel stop you from looking horizontally at the scale.

The easy, accurate way is to float the hydrometer in a clear glass or plastic cylinder. You can buy this hydrometer testing jar where you get the hydrometer. Here is the procedure:

1. Take from the fermentor enough wort to fill the testing jar about 3/4 full. (For transferring these samples, the handiest thing is a kitchen gravy baster.)

2. Float the hydrometer in the testing jar. You will notice that a number of small air bubbles stick to the instrument. These would cause considerable errors, so dislodge them by spinning the instrument briskly with a twist of thumb and forefinger. Let it spin in the liquid for a few seconds, then steady it again.

3. Place your eye level with the surface of the liquid. You will see that surface tension causes the liquid to climb a little way up the stem of the hydrometer, forming a tiny curve called the meniscus. Ignore the meniscus, and see where the liquid, if it were level, would intersect the stem; read the scale at this point.

4. If necessary, apply the temperature correction. Each hydrometer is calibrated to read accurately at one temperature – many at 60°F., some at 68°F. If the liquid is more than two or three degrees above or below the standard temperature, the reading will be significantly out. There may be a

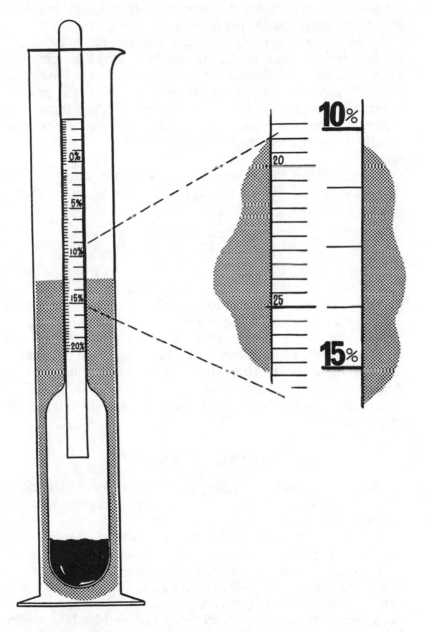

Hydrometer

temperature correction table supplied with your hydrometer. If not, consult the one at the back of this book.

5. After the test, carefully wash and dry the hydrometer, jar and baster. Lack of cleanliness here could contaminate your brew the next time you use the hydrometer. Moreover, if your hydrometer is not scrupulously clean, it will give inaccurate readings. Even the natural oil exuding from your hands is enough to cause errors, so you would do well to handle the instrument with a clean cloth, not with your bare fingers.

Recommended hydrometer readings for the start, and for various stages of the production process, are set out with the recipes in following chapters.

NON-FERMENTABLE SOLIDS

In beermaking, the malt contains a considerable amount of non-fermentable solids – coloring and flavoring substances that are not converted to alcohol. Finished beer, because it contains all these dissolved solids, will very rarely have an S.G. below 1.000. Beer containing extra malt will tend to have a somewhat higher terminal S.G., despite the extra alcohol it contains. Beers with extra sugar and little malt, such as Austrian lager, will tend to have low terminal S.G. If you go on to experiment with your own recipes, it will be well to bear this point in mind.

A CAUTIONARY TALE

In case you think I am harping too much on this subject, read and ponder this true story of a home-brewer who did not bother with sugar control.

A Texan acquaintance of mine named Mac found, during the Great Depression, that he could no longer make a living as a cowhand. But he reasoned that even if (or maybe because) people couldn't afford to eat good beef, they were still dying; so he decided to become an undertaker. He apprenticed himself to an experienced mortician, and his boss kindly let him live at the funeral parlor, in a room above the chapel.

Mac found his new profession a little depressing, and his tiny wages would not pay for liquor, so he began brewing beer in his room. Using hit-or-miss methods, he managed to produce a beverage that could be forced down, if it was thoroughly chilled, and that contained enough alcohol to cheer him up. And, most important, it was cheap. As time went on, he achieved some local fame as a beermaker, and his friends began to ask his advice on ingredients and recipes.

One hot summer afternoon Mac was in the chapel, assisting at the funeral service of a local banker who had recently gone to face his final audit. The preacher, in his eulogy, indicated that the deceased was already in heaven, looking down benevolently on his friends below. His upward gaze and raised hand turned the mourners' eyes toward the ceiling. At this moment there was a series of sharp explosions in the room above. A brown liquid began to pour down the walls of the chapel, and there arose the unmistakable odor of fermenting beer.

Mac, the only one immediately aware of what had happened, quietly slipped from the chapel during the confusion and, without waiting to be tarred and feathered, gathered up his boots and saddle and rode off rapidly into the sunset.

5. Let's Brew

Warning: It can be hazardous to alter recipes for sparkling beverages! I strongly recommend that all recipes be followed to the letter until you have gained considerable experience, and a thorough understanding of the fermentation process.

Above all, do not increase the sugar content in relation to the volume of water. Do not put the beverage prematurely into bottles. Do not attempt to get more sparkle or a better head by increasing the quantities of sugar or syrup added at the time of bottling.

A bursting bottle is no joke; it is a bomb. It can kill you, or one of your children or friends. So *be careful and be safe!*

THE BASIC PROCESS

This chapter begins with step-by-step instructions for making 5 gallons of light lager. Brewing methods are much the same for most of the recipes that follow, so there will be no need to repeat all the instructions every time. In those later recipes I shall go into detail only where you need to make some departure from the basic process.

Note: All teaspoon and tablespoon measures are *level* spoonfuls.

51

No. 1. LIGHT LAGER

❊

1 2½-lb can Brewmaster extra pale malt extract
2 oz brewing hops, Cluster or Brewer's Gold
½ oz Kent finishing hops
2½ lb corn sugar
5 gallons water
2 tsp salt
1 tsp citric acid
1 tsp Vita-Vin *or* 1 tsp brewing salts
½ tsp fining gelatin
1 tsp heading liquid
1 tsp ascorbic acid
Pure lager yeast starter

1. Get some pure lager yeast. This is a bottom yeast whose scientific name is *Saccharomyces carlsbergensis*. It is anaerobic; that is, it needs very little oxygen. This property of lager yeast requires that you take special precautions, at every stage of lager production, to exclude air as much as possible, and so avoid oxidation of the beer. Oxidation makes lager darker in color and tends to give it a harsh flavor, quite unlike the enjoyable bitterness of the hops. So keep the primary fermentor closely covered; keep the secondary fermentor well filled up, and the fermentation lock in place all the time the beer is in the vessel; in siphoning, bottling and all other operations, move the beer as gently as you can, because all splashing and needless agitation gives it the chance to absorb more oxygen. These precautions apply to the making of all beers.

Prepare a strong, actively fermenting starter, following the instructions in Chapter 3. Don't skimp on the starter; make at least a quart, preferably more. Wait till the starter is ready for use before you proceed any further.

2. It is best to boil all the water that you are going to use. If your boiler will not hold it all, boil as much of it as you can – certainly not less than one gallon.

3. When the water is boiling, add the malt extract, stirring frequently to prevent scorching.

4. Tie up the brewing hops in a straining bag or in cheese-cloth and put into the boiler. (If the hops are compressed, break them up first.)

5. Add the salt and citric acid.

6. Cover the boiler to reduce evaporation, and keep the liquid simmering for one to two hours. Stir it regularly to help extract the hop flavor and to prevent scorching.

7. Meanwhile put the corn sugar into your primary fermentor, keeping back just enough to use later in bottling — 2 ounces per gallon.

8. When time is up for the boiling, take out the bag of brewing hops, squeeze out as much of the liquid as you can, and throw the hops away.

9. Pour the hot wort into the primary fermentor, and stir thoroughly to dissolve every bit of the sugar. If you could not boil all the water, add the rest of the cold water to the primary fermentor.

10. Throw the finishing hops loose into the wort and stir so that they are thoroughly moistened.

11. Cover the fermentor with sheet plastic, well tied down, and wait till the wort has cooled to 65°F. or lower. If you boiled all the water, this cooling will take at least 12 hours.

12. Remove the cover and add your yeast starter. Be sure to shake the starter bottle so that you pour out all the sediment.

13. At this stage you want to measure what we call the starting gravity – that is, the S.G. of the wort at the start of fermentation – and adjust it if necessary. With a gravy baster draw off some wort into your hydrometer testing jar, and read its specific gravity. For this recipe the starting gravity should be 1.028 to 1.030. If it is above or below these limits, correct it. If too low, add sugar; if too high, add water. When correcting S.G., add the sugar or water *a little at a time,* stir to mix it thoroughly, and test again with the hydrometer.

(The reason why the S.G. may need adjusting is that you cannot tell in advance just how much sugar there will be in your malt extract; you cannot tell, either, just how much of the original volume of water you lost during the boiling of the wort. It is well worth the slight effort needed to get the starting gravity correct.)

14. Replace and tie down the plastic sheet, and leave the wort to ferment at a temperature of about 55° to 65°F. This is the primary fermentation.

15. After three or four days, test the S.G. and keep testing daily till it falls to 1.020. Then skim off the finishing hops and throw them away. Siphon the brew into the secondary fermentor. Add the Vita-Vin or brewing salts.

16. Put the fining gelatin into a cup of cold water and let it stand for half an hour. Then bring it to the boil, stirring gently until the gelatin is completely dissolved. Let the solution stand until it is cool to the touch, then pour it into the carboy, stirring gently with the handle of your spoon or with a clean stick to distribute the finings through the bulk of the beer.

17. Apply the fermentation lock to the carboy. There should be about three inches between the bottom of the fermentation lock and the surface of the liquid. If necessary, top up the brew to this level with sterile water (boiled and cooled under cover). If you have too much beer at this time, temporarily place the surplus in a half-gallon jug with a fermentation lock.

18. Leave the beer for at least a week to ferment in a dark place, at a constant temperature between 40° and 50°F. The lower the temperature within this range, the longer the secondary fermentation will take, but the better will be the finished beer. After a week, read S.G. every few days to see whether it has fallen to the terminal level of 1.000. At the same time, see whether the beer is getting clear. In a cool place, this may take three weeks; but don't worry. The beer is aging, and you are losing no time, for if it does not age in the carboy, it must age in the bottle.

19. When the beer has reached terminal gravity and is reasonably clear, bottle it, adding either sugar or syrup to get a renewed fermentation in the bottles that will produce the

desired amount of gas. Also add the ascorbic acid and the heading liquid. At this time you can sweeten and bottle any surplus that was set aside at Stage 17. (For full details on sweetening, bottling and storage, see Chapter 7.)

20. Store the bottles in a dark, cool place. After two weeks, put a bottle in the refrigerator for half an hour to chill, and try the result of your labors. It should taste quite good at this stage, but the rest of the beer will continue to improve for another three or four months.

I know there has been a widespread belief that beer is good only for three or four weeks' storage; but I have determined by repeated tests that home-brew, carefully made – especially where hops are used – and stored reasonably cool, will keep for six to twelve months. Certainly, after three months' aging it is a vastly better beverage than it was after three weeks!

No. 2. MEDIUM LAGER

❈

This recipe yields a beer identical in appearance with the light lager, but with a slightly higher alcoholic content.

1 2½-lb can Brewmaster extra
  pale malt extract
2 oz brewing hops, Cluster or
  Brewer's Gold
½ oz Kent finishing hops
3½ lbs corn sugar
5 gallons water
2 tsp salt

1 tsp citric acid
1 tsp Vita-Vin *or* 1 tsp brewing
  salts
½ tsp fining gelatin
1 tsp heading liquid
1 tsp ascorbic acid
Pure lager yeast starter

Processing methods are the same as for the light lager, except that in this case the starting gravity should be between 1.035 and 1.040 (because of the extra sugar). Terminal gravity, as before, should be 1.000.

No. 3. HEAVY-BODIED STRONG LAGER

This recipe gives the equivalent of Pilsener beer.

2 2-lb cans light malt extract
2 oz brewing hops, Cluster or Brewer's Gold
½ oz Kent finishing hops
4 lb corn sugar
5 gallons water
2 tsp salt
1 tsp citric acid
1 tsp Vitá-Vin *or* 1 tsp brewing salts
1 tsp fining gelatin
1 tsp heading liquid
1 tsp ascorbic acid
Pure lager yeast starter

Process this in the same way as the other lagers. Starting gravity is 1.043 to 1.045, terminal gravity 1.003.

Mature this in bottle for four to six months, and you'll have an exceptionally good beer.

No. 4. BREW-ART LAGER BEER

❊

This produces a full-bodied, true lager-style beer.

4 lb Edme D.M.S. Malt Extract
1 lb crystal malt
5 gallons water
2 oz compressed hops *or* 4 oz hop
    extract
½ oz Kent finishing hops
2 lb corn sugar

1 level tsp citric acid
1½ level tsp household salt
1 tsp brewing salts *or* ½ tsp yeast
    energizer
½ tsp gelatin finings
1 tsp ascorbic acid
1 tsp heading liquid
Pure lager yeast starter

Starting gravity is 1.038 to 1.045. Terminal gravity is 1.000.

To use the crystal malt, first crush it with a coffee grinder, food grinder or rolling-pin.

Process in the same way as the other lagers, boiling crystal malt with malt extract and water.

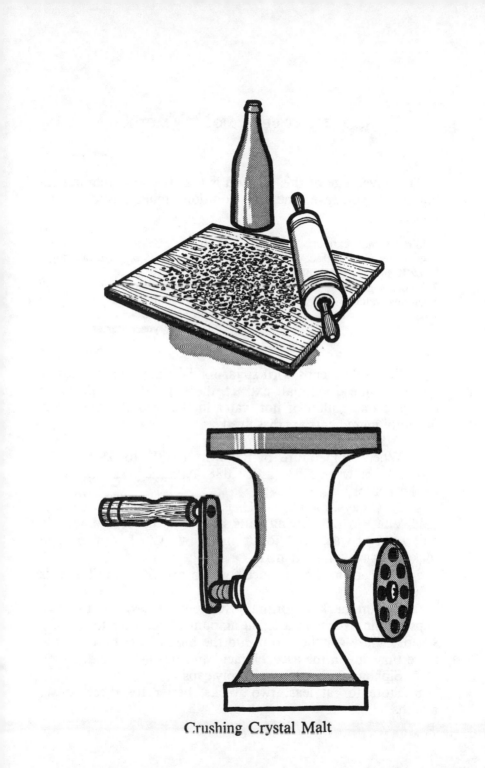

Crushing Crystal Malt

No. 5. LIGHT BEER, MODERN METHOD

❁

The advantage of this method is that the wort requires no boiling; so you save time, and you don't make a smell in the house.

3 lb dried malt extract
1 4-oz can Hop Extract
½ oz Kent hops (optional)
2 lb corn sugar
5 gallons water
1 tsp salt

1 tsp citric acid
1 tsp Vita-Vin *or* 1 tsp brewing
  salts
½ tsp beer finings
1 tsp heading liquid
1 tsp ascorbic acid
Pure lager yeast starter

1. Set aside 2 cups corn sugar for bottling. Put the rest of the sugar, the dried malt extract, the hop extract, salt, citric acid and one gallon of hot water in the primary fermentor. Stir until ingredients are dissolved.

2. Add the remainder of the water, cold.

3. When temperature of the wort is 60° to 65°F., S.G. should be between 1.035 and 1.038. Add the yeast and cover the fermentor.

4. In 6 days, or when S.G. is 1.010, siphon into carboy. Add Vita-Vin or brewing salts. Dissolve the beer finings in half a cup of water and add to the brew. Attach fermentation lock. See page 54 — item 16.

5. Ferment in a cool place for two weeks, or until S.G. is 1.000.

6. Siphon back to primary fermentor. Dissolve the two cups bottling sugar in a small amount of the beer to make a syrup. Gently stir the syrup into the bulk of the beer. At the same time stir in the ascorbic acid and heading liquid.

7. Siphon into bottles and apply caps.

8. Store for at least two weeks, better for three to six months.

No. 6. DARK BEER, MODERN METHOD

❉

Use the same procedure as for No. 4, but substitute dark malt extract in the recipe.

No. 7. AUSTRIAN LIGHT LAGER

❀

This interesting recipe we obtained from one of our Austrian customers.

½ lb crystal malt
10 gallons water
8 lb corn sugar
2½ lb of light malt extract,
   hop flavored
4 oz brewing hops, Cluster or
   Brewer's Gold
1½ oz Kent finishing hops

2 tsp Vita-Vin
1 tsp brewing salts
2 tsp salt
1 tsp citric acid
2 tsp ascorbic acid
2 tsp finings
½ vial heading liquid
1 pkg beer yeast

1. Make half a gallon of starter with two envelopes of yeast, 24 hours before you begin preparing the wort.

2. Crush the crystal malt in a coffee grinder or food grinder, or under a rolling-pin.

3. Boil the crushed crystal malt, malt extract and brewing hops in as much of the water as possible for one hour, then pour over the sugar in the primary fermentor (except for 2-1/2 cups of sugar that you hold back for later use in bottling).

4. While the wort is hot, add the finishing hops.

5. Add cold water to make up to the required total volume.

6. Stir in the salt, Vita-Vin and citric acid.

7. When the temperature falls to 65°F. add yeast starter.

8. Cover and ferment 3 days at 60° to 65°F.

9. After 3 days remove finishing hops, siphon into secondary fermentor, add finings and brewing salts, apply fermentation lock and put in a cool place for the secondary fermentation.

10. After 10 days, or when S.G. is 1.000, siphon into primary fermentor. Add the heading liquid and ascorbic acid. With a little of the beer and the 2-1/2 cups bottling sugar, make a syrup and stir it gently into the bulk of the beer. Siphon into beer bottles and crown cap.

11. Bottle and age for at least 2 months.

No. 8. BREW-ART LIGHT BEER

This recipe yields a light-bodied domestic style beer.

2 lb Edme D.M.S. Malt
5 gallons water
2 oz compressed hops *or* 4 oz hop extract
½ oz Kent finishing hops
3 lb corn sugar
1 tsp citric acid
1½ tsp household salt
1 tsp brewing salts or ½ tsp yeast energizer
½ tsp gelatin finings
1 tsp ascorbic acid
1 tsp heading liquid
Pure lager yeast starter

Starting gravity should be 1.038 to 1.045, terminal gravity 1.000.

Process in the same way as Lager No. 1.

ALE

❈

For ale – as for all other beers except lager – we use aerobic yeast that rises to the top of the brew and needs a good supply of oxygen to do its work. Ale yeast ferments at a higher temperature than lager yeast – up to 60°F. This special yeast, together with the extra hops customarily used, gives the finished ale its characteristic bitter tang.

Of course, you could cut down on hops and sugar to give a milder-tasting drink of lower alcoholic content, but then you would have something that was not really ale. Most people who prefer ale are looking for the extra flavor and the extra 1% to 2% alcohol that distinguish ale from the lighter beers.

Here are three general rules for making good ale.

1. Employ a good quality brewing hop, and be sure you use enough of it.

2. Use enough sugar to give an alcohol content of 5% to 8% by volume.

3. Give the finished ale extra time in the bottle to mature the extra alcohol.

Now let's look at some recipes.

No. 9. PALE LIGHT-BODIED ALE

❊

1 2-lb can light malt extract
2 oz brewing hops, Cluster or
   Brewer's Gold
½ oz Kent finishing hops
4 lb corn sugar
5 gallons water
1 tsp salt

3 tsp water treatment
1 tsp citric acid
1 tsp Vita-Vin *or* 1 tsp brewing
   salts
½ tsp fining gelatin
1 tsp heading liquid
1 tsp ascorbic acid
Pure ale yeast starter

Note: Add water treatment to boiling wort.

Process in the same way as lager, except that you regularly stir the primary fermentor, and conduct the secondary fermentation at a temperature between 50° and 60°F.

Starting gravity is 1.033 to 1.035. Terminal gravity is 1.000.

Mature this ale in bottle for six to ten weeks.

No. 10. DARK ALE, LIGHT-BODIED

❊

Use dark malt extract, but otherwise proceed exactly as with Recipe No. 9.

No. 11. MEDIUM PALE ALE, HEAVY-BODIED

❀

This requires the same ingredients and processing as with Recipe No. 9, except that you use *two* cans of plain light malt extract.

Starting gravity will be about 1.045, terminal gravity about 1.002 or 1.003.

Let this mature at least three months in the bottle to get best results from the recipe.

No. 12. DARK BITTER ALE

❀

Extra brewing hops and the replacement of some corn sugar by dark brown sugar give this ale a distinctive flavor.

1 2½-lb can plain dark malt extract
4 oz brewing hops, Brewer's Gold
½ oz Kent finishing hops
3 lb corn sugar
1 lb brown sugar
5 gallons water
2 tsp salt

1 tsp citric acid
3 tsp water treatment
1 tsp Vita-Vin *or* 1 tsp brewing salts
1 tsp heading liquid
1 tsp ascorbic acid
Pure ale yeast starter

Note: Add water treatment to boiling wort.

Process the same as the other ales. Starting gravity is 1.040. Terminal gravity is 1.000.

No. 13. STRONG DARK ALE, HEAVY-BODIED

⚙

2 2½-lb cans plain dark malt
  extract
3 oz brewing hops, Brewer's Gold
½ oz Kent finishing hops
3 lb corn sugar
1 lb brown sugar
1 lb crystal malt
5 gallons water
2 tsp salt

1 tsp citric acid
2 tbsp molasses
3 tsp water treatment
⅛ stick licorice
1 tsp Vita-Vin *or* 1 tsp brewing
  salts
1 tsp heading liquid
1 tsp ascorbic acid
Pure ale yeast starter

Freeze and pulverize the licorice and add it to the boiling wort when you add the brewing hops.

Starting gravity is 1.050. Terminal gravity is 1.004 to 1.006.

Age at least 3 months in bottle; 6 months' aging is better. and this ale will keep for a year or two.

No. 14.   OLD COUNTRY STYLE ALE

❧

1 lb crystal malt
1 2½-lb can John Bull dark malt
3 oz brewing hops, Cluster or
    Brewer's Gold
½ oz Kent finishing hops
3 lb corn sugar
1 oz gypsum

5 gallons water
1 tsp Vita-Vin *or* 1 tsp brewing
    salts
½ tsp beer finings
1 tsp heading liquid
1 tsp ascorbic acid
Pure ale yeast starter

Starting gravity, 1.038 to 1.040. Terminal gravity, 1.000. Save two cups of sugar for bottling.

Grind up the crystal malt before brewing in a food or a coffee grinder, or under a rolling pin.

The gypsum is included in the initial brewing, when you boil the crystal malt, malt extract and brewing hops for one hour.

Otherewise proceed as with other ales.

Note: If you like a less gassy ale, use only one cup of sugar for bottling.

No. 15. BREW-ART PALE ALE

❊

This yields a full-bodied, strong ale.

4 lb Edme S.F.X. malt
1 lb crystal malt
5 gallons water
2 oz compressed hops *or* 4 oz hop
  extract
½ oz Kent finishing hops
2 lb corn sugar
1 tsp citric acid

1 tsp salt
1 tsp brewing salts *or* ½ tsp yeast
  energizer
½ tsp gelatin finings
1 tsp ascorbic acid
1 tsp heading liquid
1 oz gypsum
Pure ale yeast starter

Starting gravity should be 1.038 to 1.045, terminal gravity 1.000.

Process in the same way as No. 14.

No. 16. BREW-ART LIGHT ALE

꘎

This recipe yields a fine, light-bodied ale.

2 lb Edme S.F.X. malt extract
5 gallons water
2 oz compressed hops *or* 4 oz hop
  extract
½ oz. Kent finishing hops
3 lb corn sugar
1 tsp citric acid

1½ tsp salt
1 tsp brewing salts *or* ½ tsp yeast
  energizer
½ tsp gelatin finings
1 tsp ascorbic acid
1 tsp heading liquid
Pure ale yeast starter

(*N.B.:* 2 lb Edme hopped S.F.X. may be used instead of the S.F.X. malt and compressed hops.)

Starting gravity should be 1.038 to 1.045, terminal gravity 1.000.

Process in the same way as No. 9.

No. 17. STOUT

1 2-lb can Stout wort
1 oz brewing hops, Brewer's Gold
½ oz Kent finishing hops
4 lb corn sugar
1 lb crystal malt
5 gallons water
1 tsp salt
2 tsp water treatment

1 tsp citric acid
1 tsp Vita-Vin or 1 tsp brewing
salts
⅛ stick licorice
1 tsp heading liquid
1 tsp ascorbic acid
Pure stout yeast starter

1. Crush the crystal malt (not too fine). It is not necessary to convert starches to fermentable sugar. Crystal malt has been carried one step further than regular malted barley.

2. Break up the Brewer's Gold hops and tie them in cheesecloth. Freeze and pulverize the licorice.

3. Using as much water as your boiler permits safely, add the crystal malt, stout wort extract, brewing hops, citric acid, salt, water treatment and licorice. Bring to a gentle boil, simmer for one to two hours, then throw out the brewing hops.

4. From here on, proceed just as you did with ale. Starting gravity is 1.040 to 1.045. Terminal gravity is 1.005. Primary fermentation should be at 60° to 65°F.; secondary fermentation at 55° to 60°F.

5. Age in bottle for at least one month. This stout will keep in bottle for a year or more.

6. Cider and Perry

Cider and perry are wines of moderate alcoholic content (about 8% to 10% by volume) made from the juice of the apple and the pear respectively. They can be made sparkling by the same process of bottle fermentation that produces the head on beer. Or, if you prefer, you can make still (*i.e.*, non-sparkling) cider and perry.

If you live in an area where grapes won't ripen, you will particularly enjoy the economy and the personal satisfaction of using your own home-grown fruit to make cider and perry.

Apple and pear juices are rather delicate, and need careful handling to avoid oxidation that would spoil their color. But, with the simple precautions described in this chapter, you can be sure of making a superb light beverage.

This subject takes me back over the years, to the first time I took my wife to Mexico for the winter. I could say that was when Mexico was still Mexico; but we were both in our twenties, so it might be closer to the truth to say that was when Anderson was still Anderson. We were in Mexico City when a few friendly members of the American Embassy staff invited us to help celebrate New Year's Eve. I believe we cemented Canadian-U.S. relations quite firmly that evening. The cement we were using was premium quality French champagne. It was my wife's first taste of this wine, and I've never forgotten her remark, delivered with all her charming, youthful innocence: "Gee, I didn't know they made champagne from apples."

There was nothing wrong with her taste buds; many people have noticed the similarity between brut champagne and top-quality cider. Make some good cider, age it properly, then try the blindfold test with your friends. You will find that most of them cannot distinguish your cider from champagne.

SELECTING FRUIT

You can make perfectly good cider from whatever apples you have in your garden; but, if you want to experiment with obtaining subtly different flavors, you should try blending sweet and bitter apples – for example, Macintosh and Delicious with Spartan or Northern Spy. You may be able to trade some of your own apples with a neighbor who has different varieties; or, if you live in an area where there are commercial orchards, you may be able to buy culls. The culls are serviceable so long as they are not bruised or mouldy.

The same principle applies in blending pears for perry. Note that ripe fruit, or fruit that has been picked and left to stand for a few days, will yield its juice more readily than unripe, fresh-picked fruit, and will usually produce better-tasting perry or cider.

CRUSHING

To get juice from apples or pears, you first crush the fruit – that is, shred it into pulp – and then put the pulp into a press to squeeze the juice out of it. I emphasize this dual process because I find some people think they can press the fruit without crushing it first.

It's important to use a proper apple or pear crusher for this process. Apples or pears are much harder than grapes, so if you try to put them through a grape crusher you will break the machine.

Prevent Oxidation

You can easily see that during crushing and pressing the fruit pulp and juice unavoidably get a thorough exposure to air. So, to avoid unpleasant discoloration of the juice and

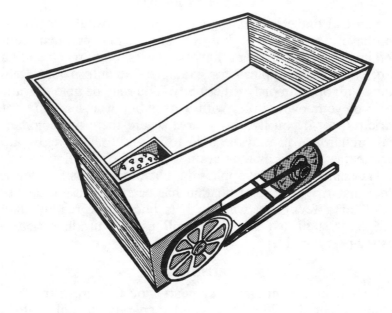

Apple Crusher

impairment of flavor, you will want to take precautions against oxidation.

For each 50 pounds of fruit you have to process, dissolve 1/2 level teaspoon of potassium metabisulphite or sodium metabisulphite, plus 1/2 level teaspoon of an antioxidant such as ascorbic acid or sodium erythorbate, in 1 cup of water. (*E.g.*, for 200 lb fruit you use 2 tsp metabisulphite and 2 tsp antioxidant in 4 cups water.)

Place the solution in a sprinkler-bottle, such as is used for sprinkling clothes prior to ironing. Any other convenient sprinkling device will do, but it must be of glass or plastic, because the metabisulphite will react with metal.

Sprinkle the solution liberally on the fruit as fast as it comes from the machine, and mix it in thoroughly with a wooden spoon.

This treatment will give about 75 parts per million of sulphur dioxide in the freshly crushed apples or pears. By the time the pulp has been pressed and the bulk of the solids thrown away, the pure juice will contain less than 25 parts per million. If you neglect or bungle these antioxidant precautions, no amount of time and trouble spent on subsequent stages of processing will yield a first-class beverage. If properly carried out, this treatment will effectively preserve the color and flavor of the juice.

Pectic Enzyme

As the fruit comes from the crusher is the best time, too, to add the pectic enzyme. This will make the pulp release more juice when it is pressed and, later on, will help to clarify the beverage during and after secondary fermentation.

Use 1/2 tsp for each 20 lb of fruit. Sprinkle the powder over the crushed fruit, or make a slurry with the powder and a little juice and sprinkle that. Either way, the enzyme will at once go to work breaking down the pectin to release more juice and flavor.

PRESSING

Cider presses, specifically designed for apples, were for a long time just about unobtainable. Moreover the apple pulp has to be placed in cloth bags for pressing, and ordinary cloth bags were not strong enough to withstand the high pressures required to extract all the juice from apples or pears. Now the situation is much improved due to the availability of strong, reuseable nylon straining bags, and there's nothing to prevent the home winemaker from producing abundant supplies of apple and pear juice.

Cellulose Fiber

Commercial processors of apple and pear juice usually add cellulose fiber to the pulp before pressing. This is a chemically purified fiber made from wood, and it undoubtedly helps to release more juice from the fruit.

The fiber comes in different grades, with full instructions for use on the packages. In the U.S.A. one brand name is Solka-Floc.

This cellulose fiber is not yet available everywhere, but probably will become more widely distributed as home winemakers recognize its advantages. So ask for it at your homebrew supply store.

Medium Quantities

The grape presses sold at winemakers' supply stores will effectively handle apple pulp if you have only a few score pounds to press.

The typical press, made of hardwood or enamelled steel, has three main parts: a basket-like container, a screw-driven plunger and a tray to collect the expressed juice. Such a press will take 20 to 40 pounds of apple or pear pulp at a time.

1. Raise the screw to its maximum height and remove the plunger.

2. If you are using a small press, place the pulp in a nylon straining bag. For bigger presses, use nylon press cloths to wrap the pulp. (Cotton or linen cloths can be used, but they are harder to clean than nylon, wear out sooner and release the juice more slowly than nylon.) Make sure that the top of the bagged pulp is level, then replace the plate.

3. Apply pressure *slowly* until you feel a fair resistance, then wait five or ten minutes while juice runs out the bottom of the press.

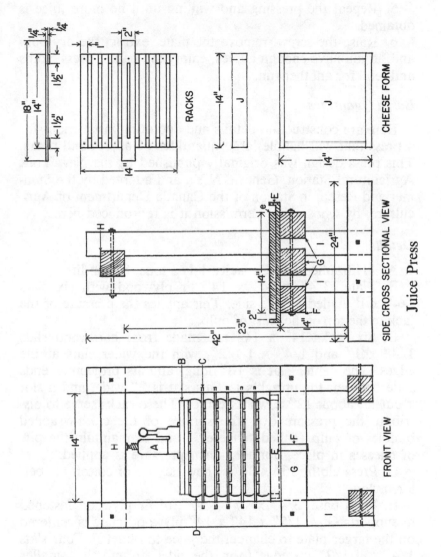

RACKS

CHEESE FORM

Juice Press

SIDE CROSS SECTIONAL VIEW

FRONT VIEW

4. Screw down a little farther and wait again while more juice runs out.

5. Repeat the pressing and waiting until no more juice is obtained.

6. Raise the screw, remove the plate, extract the dry pulp and, if you have enough apples, empty the bag or press cloths and refill for another run.

Large Quantities

Here are construction details and operating instructions for a press that will handle large quantities of apples and pears. This press design was originally published by the New York Agricultural Station, Geneva, N.Y., and adapted by the Summerland Research Station of the Canada Department of Agriculture, by whose kind permission it is reproduced here.

Details

A. Hydraulic jack. Capacity 1-1/2 tons, 8 inch lift.

B. Plate, 3/4" x 14" x 14" fir plywood with six slats 1/4" x 1" nailed on one side. This applies the pressure of the jack to the top of the mass of pulp.

C. Six racks 14" x 14" are made from hardwood slats 1/4" x 1" and 1/4" x 1-1/2", with the wider slats at the edges. The center slat is 18" long, and its projecting ends slide between the uprights I. This slat is 2" wide, and a slot is cut for about 12" down its center. These racks serve to distribute the pressure over the surface of the cloth-wrapped bundles of pulp (called "cheeses") and to maintain the pile of cheeses in place, upright, when pressure is applied.

D. Press cloth, 36" x 36". They may be of cotton or, better, nylon.

E. Press base, 3/4" x 17" x 17", of fir plywood fastened to supports G. A 1/2" x 14" x 14" plywood plate is centered on the larger plate to channel the juice to outlet F. Four slats 1/4" x 1-1/2" on edge form the sides around this smaller plate.

F. Juice outlet, a 3/4" pipe of plastic, set in a hole in Base E.

G. Support for press base, 4" x 4", hardwood or fir.

H. Press top, 4" x 4", harwood or fir. A metal plate is fitted on its lower side at the point where the jack makes contact.

I. Uprights, 4" x 4", hardwood or fir. A reinforcement of 1/4" x 4" metal stripping should be well screwed down across the press top, and 20" down the inner side of each upright.

J. Cheese form, outer dimensions 14" x 14", made of 2" x 3/4" harwood.

Notes

1. All wooden parts of the press that come in direct contact with the juice should be coated with hot paraffin.

2. For all parts of the press that come in direct contact with the juice, stainless steel nails or screws should be used.

3. Do not try to skimp on construction of the press by using lumber of less than the recommended dimensions, or by omitting the bolts and other strengthening features indicated.

Using the Press

1. Make a cheese. Place one rack on the base of the press. Place the cheese form on the rack. Lay a press cloth over the cheese form. Pour the crushed fruit into the middle of the cloth. Under the weight of the fruit, the cloth sags down. Add fruit until it lies 2 inches deep all over the cheese form. Fold the cloth neatly in from all sides toward the center of the cheese. Take away the cheese form, and you have a neat, square, cloth-wrapped package of crushed fruit – the cheese.

2. Place another rack on top of the first cheese, and repeat the process.

3. Add another rack, another cheese, another rack, and so on, until there is just room for the jack support and jack between the top of the piled cheeses and the press top. Make sure that the jack is centered on the jack support.

4. Pump the jack, applying pressure *gradually, in stages,* as recommended earlier for small-scale press operation.

Yield

The juice content of apples and pears varies somewhat with the variety and with the season. But you can roughly estimate that 17 to 22 pounds of fruit will yield a gallon of juice.

REMOVING SOLIDS

When the juice has been pressed and collected, we treat it differently from grape juice. We postpone the primary fermentation until after the solids have settled out of the juice.

Put the freshly pressed juice into a large vessel and let it stand overnight, covered with sheet plastic. Next day most of the solids will have settled to the bottom in a layer several inches thick. This process is called keeving.

There will be enough metabisulphite left over from that which you sprinkled on the pulp to keep the juice white during keeving and to prevent the growth of spoilage bacteria.

After the solids have settled, carefully rack off the clear juice into your primary fermentor. To minimize the risk of oxidation, take every precaution to avoid splashing or otherwise agitating the juice.

No. 18. CIDER FROM FRESH APPLE JUICE

❧

Here is a recipe for 1 gallon of juice. You can adapt it for whatever quantity you may have.

1 gallon fresh apple juice   ¼ tsp Vita-Vin
Sugar to S.G. 1.060   Starter or champagne or Andovin
½ tsp acid blend   yeast
¼ tsp grape tannin

Notes

1. If the juice has been prepared as suggested earlier, it already contains pectic enzyme and metabisulphite. If you have obtained or prepared your juice in some other manner, add 1/2 tsp pectic enzyme powder, 1 Campden tablet and 1 antioxidant tablet per gallon.

2. Vita-Vin, a new product, is a very effective source of nutrition for fermentation. If you cannot get it where you live, use ordinary yeast energizer.

3. In apple juice, with no suspended solids, it is sometimes difficult to get the fermentation started, especially if the temperature is in the low 70's. So, even if using Andovin or some other prepared dry yeast, make and use a large, strong starter.

4. This recipe calls for 1/2 tsp of acid blend. This is an average amount. But if you are carrying out the acid testing procedure described later in this chapter, test the acid content of the juice before fermenting it, and adjust it to 5.5%.

Procedure

1. Prepare the juice as directed above and place it in the primary fermentor. Add cane sugar to bring the starting gravity up to 1.060.

2. Add all the other ingredients, including the yeast starter.

3. Cover with a plastic sheet, firmly tied down, and ferment at 55° to 65°F. until S.G. falls to 1.020. This should take 3 to 5 days.

4. Siphon into a gallon jug (or a carboy for larger quantities) and apply fermentation lock. Keep at 55° to 65°F.

5. When S.G. falls to 1.000 (after about 3 weeks) rack and add 1 Wine-Art antioxidant tablet per gallon.

6. When the cider becomes clear, rack again into the primary fermentor. For each gallon of cider, take 1-1/2 ounces sugar. Draw off a little of the cider and make a syrup with the sugar. Add the syrup to the bulk of the cider and stir in gently. Siphon into beer bottles and close with crown caps.

7. Age at least three months in bottle; six months will give much better results.

No. 19. PERRY FROM FRESH PEAR JUICE

❀

Proceed exactly as in Recipe No. 18, substituting fresh pear juice for apple juice.

CIDER AND PERRY FROM CONCENTRATES

❀

Perhaps you cannot easily get large quantities of apples and pears; or perhaps you have not the space, equipment or time to crush and press fruit. Then you will appreciate the saving of time and the convenience of working with apple and pear concentrates.

They are made from pure, freshly pressed juice, dehydrated in vacuum, either with or without application of heat. The degree of concentration varies somewhat, but is usually about nine to one – that is, nine gallons of fresh juice makes one gallon of concentrate.

As the concentrates have been carefully filtered to remove all solid matter, you can eliminate the keeving. Indeed, you can conduct the whole fermentation in the secondary fermentor, under a fermentation lock, and so minimize the risk of oxidation. If you decide to do this, hold back about one-fifth of the total amount of reconstituted juice and add it to the rest after the first vigorous fermentation has subsided. Then you need only rack the cider once, when fermentation is completely finished, to get it off the yeast deposit.

As with fresh juice, it is desirable to use a big, strong yeast starter, either of Andovin or of champagne yeast.

No. 20. CIDER FROM APPLE CONCENTRATE

❈

This recipe yields about 8 gallons. The procedure described here is the conventional method, using primary and secondary fermentors, but the single-fermentor method mentioned above can be used if you prefer it.

1 96-oz can Wine-Art Apple
  Concentrate
9 cans (864 oz) water
6 Campden tablets
3 tsp pectic enzyme powder
½ tsp grape tannin

1 oz acid blend
2 tsp Vita-Vin
13 oz sugar (for bottling)
2 quarts yeast starter, champagne
  or Andovin

1. Mix all ingredients, except the 13 ounces of bottling sugar, in primary fermentor and cover with plastic sheet.

2. Ferment at about 65°F. for 5 or 6 days, till S.G. falls to 1.015.

3. Siphon to secondary fermentor and apply fermentation lock.

4. When S.G. is 0.997 to 1.000 siphon back to primary fermentor. Add 6 Winc-Art antioxidant tablets. Take a little of the cider and make a syrup with the 13 ounces of sugar. Stir the syrup gently into the bulk of the cider.

5. Siphon into beer bottles, cap, and age 3 to 6 months.

No. 21. CHRISTMAS CIDER FROM APPLE CONCENTRATE

❈

This recipe produces a stronger cider, with a higher alcohol content and more pronounced apple flavor. Yield, 6 gallons.

1 96-oz can Wine-Art Apple Concentrate	½ tsp grape tannin
	3 tsp acid blend
7 cans (672 oz) water	2 tsp yeast energizer
5 Campden tablets	Starter of champagne or Andovin
2 tsp peptic enzyme powder	wine yeast

Process in the same way as with Recipe No. 20, except that the quantity of sugar required for bottling will be only 10 ounces.

CIDER BASE

❈

As fresh apples – and consequently all apple products – become more expensive, we seek means of making a given weight of fruit go a little further. With judicious addition of sugar, fruit acids and water we can produce what is called a cider base. The end product, because it is carefully balanced, is more uniform in composition than fresh juice, and yields a cider fully as good as that obtained from the pure concentrate. This recipe uses Wine-Art Cider Base, but other firms are making similar products.

84

No. 22 CIDER FROM CIDER BASE

❀

This recipe yields 5 gallons of dry, sparkling cider.

1 96-oz can Wine-Art apple
  cider base
7 cans (672 oz) water
1 oz acid blend
1 oz yeast nutrient

4 Campden tablets
½ tsp grape tannin
2 tsp pectic enzyme powder
Andovin all-purpose wine yeast

Process in the same way as the previous cider recipes. Age at least one month.

Not more than 2 oz. sugar per gallon when bottling.

No. 23 CYSER

❀

This beverage is not so well known as it deserves to be; the addition of the honey gives it a higher alcohol content than ordinary cider. The recipe produces one gallon, and you can multiply it for larger quantities.

1 gallon apple juice
8 oz (approximately) honey*
¼ tsp grape tannin
½ tsp Vita-Vin *or* yeast
  energizer

1 tsp acid blend
Starter of Andovin all-purpose
  wine yeast

* Use enough honey to bring the specific gravity of the juice up to 1.070 – no more! Exact measurement with the hydrometer is best; 8 ounces is about the amount usually required.

1. Ferment in the primary fermentor at 55° to 65° F. for 3 days.

2. Siphon into secondary fermentor, apply fermentation lock, and leave it until fermentation has completely ceased and the cyser is clear.

3. Rack into the primary fermentor. Add 2 ounces corn sugar per gallon and bottle as with cider.

No. 24 STRONG STILL CYSER

❈

This delightful variation was suggested by my old friend
F.E. Atkinson, who was head of the Department of Agriculture in Summerland, B.C. for many years.

Follow Recipe No. 23, except for the following points:

1. Add enough honey to produce an S.G. of 1.100.
2. When secondary fermentation has ceased and the cyser
is clear, rack into the primary fermentor and mix in *a little*
vermouth flavouring. Don't overdo the vermouth flavour!
3. *Add no sugar* at this stage, but bottle as a still wine, and
age at least six months.

ACID CONTROL

The juice of apples and pears always contains a certain
amount of acid, but this amount can vary widely from one
variety to another; it varies in the same variety from one
garden and from one season to another.

Juice that is deficient in acid can give you a lot of trouble:

1. It is more than usually susceptible to oxidation, with
unwanted darkening of colour and impairment of flavour.
2. Low-acid juice is highly susceptible to contamination
by vinegar and other spoilage bacteria.
3. Low-acid cider and perry do not keep well.

Excess acid makes juice more resistant to spoilage, but
tends to retard fermentation, and the finished beverage will

require an excessive period of aging before it becomes palatable.

The easy way to avoid these difficulties is to measure the acid content of your juice before fermentation, and adjust it to the correct level.

Acid Measurement Technique

You cannot measure the acid in a batch of fruit juice by tasting it, but there is a simple chemical process that will give accurate results. It utilizes a liquid called phenolphthalein, which is colourless in contact with acids but turns red in contact with an alkali.

Apple or pear juice always contains some acid, so you can add phenolphthalein without producing any colour change. Then, little by little, you add an alkaline solution of known strength, until the acid is exactly neutralized, and the sample is just on the border between acidity and alkalinity. At this stage the phenolphthalein turns pale pink. By observing how much alkali you added, you know how much acid the juice contained.

This process, known as titration, formerly required laboratory apparatus, but an economical acid-testing kit is now on the market. It contains:

A 20-cc. graduated plastic syringe with which you can precisely measure small quantities of liquid.

A small testing bottle.

A bottle of alkaline solution (sodium hydroxide, commonly called caustic soda).

A bottle of phenolphthalein colour indicator.

An eye-dropper.

Here is the procedure for testing a sample of apple or pear juice:

1. Be sure the syringe and testing bottle are clean and dry. Draw 15 cc. of juice into the syringe, and put it in the testing bottle.

2. Take a little phenlophthalein in the eye-dropper; put just three drops of it into the testing bottle. Shake gently to mix it in. There is no colour-change at this stage.

3. Wash out the syringe with water. Draw into it 10 cc. of the hydroxide solution.

4. Gently press the plunger to add 1 cc. of hydroxide to the testing bottle. A pink streak appears at the point where the hydroxide enters the juice. Gently shake the bottle and the pink colour will clear away.

5. Continue adding hydroxide 1 cc. at a time until, on shaking, the colour does not clear, but the whole sample of juice becomes a uniform pale pink. (If the initial 10 cc. of hydroxide fails to produce the colour change, take another 10 cc. into the syringe and continue.)

6. Note the number of cc. of hydroxide used. Each indicates .1% (one part per thousand) of acid as tartaric* in the juice. That is, if it takes 8 cc. of hydroxide to produce the colour change, the juice contains .8% acid as tartaric.

7. After use, throw away the sample of juice, wash out the syringe, testing bottle and eye-dropper. Keep the hydroxide and phenolphthalein bottles tightly stoppered; both solutions will deteriorate if exposed to air.

Recommended Acid Levels

Test the acid content of your apple or pear juice before you add the yeast starter. Once the juice has begun to ferment, the carbon dioxide entrapped in it will produce false readings in the acid test.

A desirable acid level for apple or pear juice is .5 to .6%.

Correcting Acid Deficiencies

To raise the acid content of a batch of juice, simply add acid blend crystals from your home-brew supply house. (If the blend is not available, tartaric acid alone will do.) It's a good idea, after adding the acid crystals and stirring them into solution to run the test again, as a check.

There's no need to be too finicky over acid levels. Half a percentage point one way or the other won't ruin your cider

---

* There are actually several acids in ripe fruit juice. For convenience of calculation we consider them as if they were all converted to tartaric acid.

or perry. But as a general principle, it's better to be a little on the high side of the target rather than on the low side.

Now here are some figures that will guide you in adding acid. A little arithmetic will tell you how much acid is needed, whatever the quantity of juice you have, and whatever its acid deficiency.

Small quantities: 1/3 ounce acid added to 1 gallon of juice raises the acid content by .3%.

Medium quantities: 1 ounce acid added to 5 gallons of juice raises the acid content by .18%.

Large quantities: 4 ounces acid added to 20 gallons of juices raises the acid content by .18%.

Correcting Excess Acid

There are several procedures for reducing excess acid, in the following order of preference:

1. Blend the high-acid juice with juice known to be low in acid, such as that from Delicious apples or the early-ripening Transparent.

2. Instead of blending two fresh juices, you can blend juice with reconstituted concentrate. The best way to determine the proportions for your blend is to take a measured sample — say a pint — of the high-acid juice and try adding measured quantities of the diluted concentrate, testing as you go, until the acidity is right. Then a little arithmetc will tell you the quantities required to blend the whole batch.

3. Wine-Art Acid Reducing Solution, containing potassium carbonate, can be used to neutralize excess acid. Instructions for the use of this solution in connection with the acid titration kit are enclosed with each package.

4. Potassium carbonate works quite well, and recent tests show that it produces no off-flavours.

5. Add water to the juice till you reduce the acidity to the desired proportion. Add sugar syrup to raise the specific gravity to the level you want, then ferment. This method is used by some commercial wineries. Obviously, it produces a thin, light beverage; but cider and perry are light anyway and many people find the extra dilution unobjectionable.

90

6. Ferment the high-acid juice as it is, then blend the finished cider or perry with a batch that is low in acid. Here again, blend a small sample first, testing flavour and acidity as you go to find the correct proportions.

7. It is possible to neutralize excess acid with precipitated chalk — that is, pure calcium carbonate. But this tends to leave an unpleasant after-taste. The method is not really satisfactory, and should be regarded as a last resort.

Note: Chilling for a few weeks at 25° to 30°F. removes excess acids from grape musts and wines, by precipitating much of the acid as cream of tartar. This process cannot be depended upon for cider and perry, because a large percentage of the acid in these beverages is malic, which is not so susceptible to precipitation by chilling as the tartaric acid in grape beverages.

Every Man to His Taste

I have suggested acid levels that will please the average palate, but you may find you like your cider and perry more or less acid than do most people. If so, adjust your production methods accordingly. If you buy, or are given, a cider or perry that particularly pleases you, save 15 cc. of it for a test of total acids, and use that as a guide for future operations.

PRESERVING APPLE JUICE

If you have more than enough apples for all the cider you want to make, you may be interested in preserving some apple juice fresh and unfermented. Here's how to go about it. The first five steps are exactly the same as for making cider, but for the sake of clarity I will list them briefly again.

1. Crush the apples.
2. Add metabisulphite solution and pectic enzyme.
3. Press out the juice.
4. Let solids settle overnight.
5. Carefully rack off the clear juice.
6. Add 3 Wine-Art stabilizer tablets per gallon, place the juice in sterile bottles and seal. Keep in a cool place.

Notes

1. It is possible to pasteurize juices by heating to 200°F. but the method described above preserves the flavor better.

2. If you wish to fortify your juice with additional vitamin C (as many commercial juices are fortified) add ascorbic acid crystals at the rate of 1/2 teaspoon per gallon immediately before bottling the juice.

3. Juice preserved in this way may throw down a slight sediment if stored for an extended time. This is merely the remains of the original apple solids, and is in no way a sign of deterioration. If you avoid shaking the bottle before opening you can retain the sediment at the bottom when you pour off the juice.

7. Bottling and Storage

You have brought your beer, cider or perry to the stage where secondary fermentation is over. But it is still far from being a finished, palatable beverage. The way it matures, for better or for worse, from now on, depends on the care with which you transfer it from the secondary fermentor into bottles, and the way you treat those full bottles. So let's examine the best and easiest ways of bottling and storage.

BEER

Preparing Bottles

Don't begin bottling until you have assembled enough bottles to finish the job. To leave the carboy standing half-empty overnight, or even for a few hours, while you hunt around for bottles and clean them, is to risk oxidation of the beer.

You will not be able to draw off every drop of beer from the secondary fermentor, because of the yeast deposit at the bottom. (That yeast need not be wasted, of course. Chapter 3 describes how to salvage it for the next brew.) But at this stage you don't want to stir up the yeast and get it into the bottles, so you accept a slight loss. You can estimate that one gallon of beer will fill 10 regular (12-ounce) bottles.

Having collected enough bottles, you want to be sure they are clean and sterile. Don't try to sterilize bottles by baking them in the oven. The heat does kill bacteria, but it also weakens the glass and heightens the risk of explosions, lost beer, and perhaps injuries.

Commercial breweries employ a chlorinated detergent that cleans and sterilizes at once. Chapter 2 describes various products that are suitable for home use.

But it's important that you rinse out of the bottles every last trace of chlorine and detergent. If chlorine remains in the bottles, it will kill the yeast, and you will have no bottle-ferment to put the sparkle and head on your beer. If only the detergent remains, the beer will ferment all right, but it will not form a good head.

There's no harm in leaving bottles wet with clean water; in fact, this makes it easier to bottle the beer, as it reduces foaming when the beer is siphoned into the bottles.

When to Bottle

To know when the beer is ready to bottle, you will have been regularly using the hydrometer to watch the beer move towards the recommended terminal gravity. When it reaches that level, there is no desperate rush; the beer is safe in the secondary fermentor under a fermentation lock, and is beginning to age. So once terminal gravity is attained, you can bottle any time at your convenience.

There are two ways of bottling, each with its advantages and disadvantages.

Bottling with Dry Sugar

When making the beer, you held back some corn sugar — 2 ounces per gallon — to be used in bottling. This sugar produces a gentle renewed fermentation that makes the beer effervescent when poured.

For the dry-sugar method, it is important to get an equal amount of sugar in each bottle. Too little will leave you with beer that is rather flat; too much may burst the bottle.

The amount needed is enough to raise the S.G. of the beer about 5 degrees S.G. or 1.4 degrees Balling. This works out at a little less than a level teaspoon per bottle. It is easy to pour it into the bottles through a small funnel.

There's nothing wrong with this process except that it is laborious, and it is difficult to get just the same amount into each bottle.

Some people have contended that the dry sugar sometimes fails to dissolve, and so leaves you with flat beer. I have never encountered this problem.

The dry-sugar method has the advantage that it reduces the danger of oxidizing your beer. Lager especially is very susceptible to oxidation, which makes it taste bitter and darkens its colour.

Once the secondary fermentation has stopped, you tend to oxidize the brew every time you expose it to air. The more you stir or pour the beer, the worse will be the effects of oxidation.

Many beermakers feel that, for light lagers, the extra trouble of using dry sugar at this stage is repaid by results.

Bottling with Sugar Syrup

The easiest and quickest way of adding the bottling sugar is to make it into a syrup. Here is the procedure for an average-size batch.

1. Siphon two pints of beer from the carboy, warm it in a saucepan of glass, enamel or stainless steel, and dissolve in the required quantity of corn sugar to make a syrup — 2 ounces per gallon.

2. Carefully, so as not to disturb the sediment, siphon the rest of the beer from the carboy back into the primary fermentor.

3. Add the sugar syrup, head liquid, and antioxidant, stirring gently to distribute it thoroughly through the beer.

4. Check the specific gravity of the beer. The syrup should have raised it by 5 degrees. For example, if the terminal gravity in the secondary fermentor was 1.000, the S.G. after adding syrup should be 1.005. If you have raised the S.G.

more than this, adjust it downward by adding water; if it is too low, make and add a little more syrup.

5. Immediately siphon the beer into bottles, filling them to within one inch of the top. Close them with a crown capping machine.

Here are a few notes on the syrup process. The method is easy and effects a perfectly even distribution of the sugar throughout the brew, so you have no flat or excessively gassy bottles. There is some risk of oxidation in moving the beer about in this method, but you can minimize it.

Stir as gently as possible consistent with effectively distributing the sugar syrup. Add an antioxidant. Ascorbic acid, powdered or in crystals, is good. One teaspoon is the quantity for 5 gallons. Even better is sodium erythorbate, an isomer of ascorbic acid that does not have the vitamin C content, but is a more powerful antioxidant. Use this in the same quantities as ascorbic acid.

Storage

For the first week after bottling, store your beer in a dark place at a temperature of about 60°F. while the bottle-fermentation produces the desired amount of gas. After that, storage in a cooler place would tend to make the beer keep longer. Normal-strength lager keeps well at average cellar temperatures – 45° to 60°F. The cooler the storage, the longer it keeps.

Always keep beer in the dark. Light tends to spoil its color and flavor.

I realize that most people are not interested in how long their beer will keep, but rather in how soon they can drink it. Ten to 14 days after bottling, you can take a trial drink. One bottle, well chilled before serving, will satisfy you that the batch has turned out well. Some people go on drinking the beer at this stage, but I personally don't recommend too much haste. The beer will taste better after 3 months in bottle and, if well made, will still be in excellent condition after 6 months.

Ale will keep longer than beer, particularly the stronger varieties. As a general rule, you can say that the higher the alcoholic content of a beverage, the longer it takes to mature to prime drinking quality, but the longer it will keep without deterioration.

All the same, there is no special merit in making a hundred gallons of beer at once and keeping it a long time. Many wine-makers produce one big batch of wine a year, at the time of the grape harvest. That is because grapes soon go bad. But barley and malt can be stored indefinitely, so the best way to make beer is in a series of medium-sized batches all round the calendar. That way, you never have too much processing to do at once, you always have some fairly new beer maturing, and some ready to drink.

CIDER AND PERRY

For sparkling cider and perry, bottle and store exactly as for beer, except that, to produce the bottle-fermentation, you add only 1 1/2 ounces of sugar per gallon, in the form of syrup. To make and mix the syrup, follow the directions for bottling beer earlier in this chapter.

For bottling still cider and perry, you do not need beer or soft-drink bottles, because there will be no internal pressure. Simply siphon straight out of the secondary fermentor into ordinary wine bottles and close them with corks or screw tops. With still cider and perry there is no need for the week's storage at 60°F. Simply put the bottles into a cool storage place at about 40° to 50°F. and leave them for three months or more.

8. Various Operations

Good ingredients and well-balanced recipes are half the battle in making good fermented beverages. But much depends on your correct performance of various processes. Let's examine some of these and see the easiest and best ways to do them.

RACKING

As your beer, cider or perry goes through the stages of fermentation, solids are being deposited at the bottom of the vessel. These may be such things as spent hops, fragments of cereal grains, particles of apple or pear pulp, or yeast cells. Whatever the sediment may be, you don't want to leave it too long in contact with the beverage, or it will begin to decompose and produce unwelcome flavors.

The process of removing the liquid and leaving behind the sediment is called racking. You can never get *all* the liquid off the sediment; to strive for the last few ounces would involve disturbing and carrying over at least part of the solid matter. But the slight loss of liquid at each racking is a small price to pay for a clear, better-tasting, longer-keeping beverage.

1. Take your siphon tube and tie it to a clean stick so that the stick projects an inch or two beyond the end of the tube. The length of projection should be a little greater than the depth of the sediment.

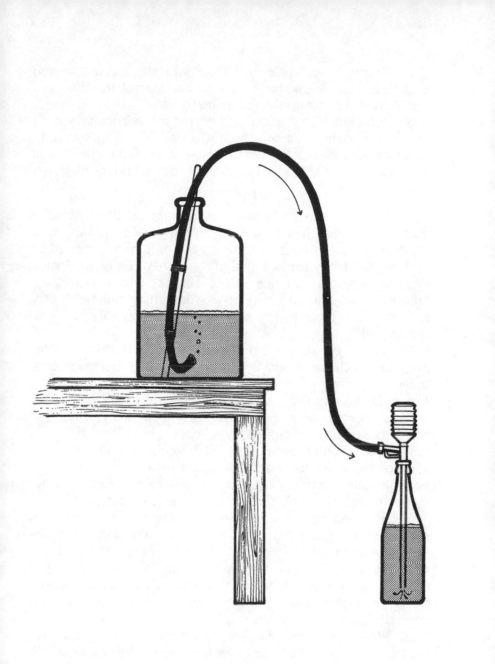

Racking

2. Gently lower stick and tube into the fermentor and start siphoning. With the stick you can control the tube and stop it from stirring up the sediment.

3. In racking lager, cider and perry, you particularly want to avoid oxidation. So put the outlet end of the siphon right down at the bottom of the carboy – or of the bottle if you are bottling – so that the liquid flows out without splashing.

FINING

You will eliminate the coarser, heavier particles of solid matter from your beer, cider or perry by racking. But some solids may be too light to settle to the bottom so, even after racking, the beverage is still slightly cloudy. To remove such material you can add one of the class of substances called finings. These have the property of attaching themselves to, and carrying down to the bottom of the fermentor, all suspended solids.

The use of gelatin for fining beer was described in Chapter 5. Gelatin will not work, by the way, unless a beverage contains enough tannin to make it floculate and settle; that is one reason for adding the grape tannin to certain recipes.

Your cider or perry may look fairly clear when it has finished its secondary fermentation, but I think you will find that the addition of finings invariably improves its clarity, and also softens it. So use finings – gelatin or a proprietary product – in your secondary fermentor a few days before bottling.

There are two precautions in connection with fining:

1. If the fining has worked well, it may have removed so much of the suspended yeast that the bottle-ferment is delayed, or even fails altogether. So, after fining and racking, at the same time as you add the bottling syrup, also mix in a starter of Andovin or champagne yeast. This ensures an adequate yeast population for the bottle ferment, but does not spoil the clarity of the cider or perry.

2. Whatever finings you use, don't try to save time by increasing the recommended quantities. Some finings, added in excess, will take the color out of your beer or cider. Worse, the excess finings may stay in suspension, leaving you with a beverage cloudier than it was before.

LABELLING

Some people like to label their beer and cider bottles with stick-on paper labels. If you want to do this, you can purchase gummed labels, with spaces for writing in the details, at most home-brew supply stores.

A cheaper, quicker method of identifying your stock is to make code marks of letters and numbers on the crown caps of the bottles. A grease pencil or felt pen will write easily enough on the smooth metal surface.

SERVING

If you drink your beer too cold – for example by gulping it from the neck of a well-refrigerated bottle – it will not yield its best flavor. The ideal serving temperature for most beers is around 45°F., although the Austrian lager, with its high content of hops and alcohol, is often served at around 35°F.

Cider and perry will taste best at 35° to 45°F.

The condition of the glass can contribute much towards giving you a satisfying drink. If you find that a batch of beer or cider has an excessively thick, active head, then rinse the glass with cold water; this will tend to prevent the drink from foaming over. If you want to make the most of the head and have it last a long time, then use a dry glass.

It is always important that the glasses be scrupulously clean. Specks of dust or lint tend to release the gas in a rush, causing a quick, excessive spurt of foam, following which the beverage quickly goes flat.

If men are being served, you may like to use one of the traditional beer mugs, with a handle on the side. Some women prefer a more delicate glass; some beer glasses used today are in the shape of wine glasses.

The important thing to remember about glasses for long drinks is that they should hold at least 15 ounces, so that you can pour a complete bottle at once and still leave room for the head of the beer or the foaming of the cider or perry.

The best way to pour is to hold the glass on a pronounced slope, place the bottle-neck against the rim of the glass, and

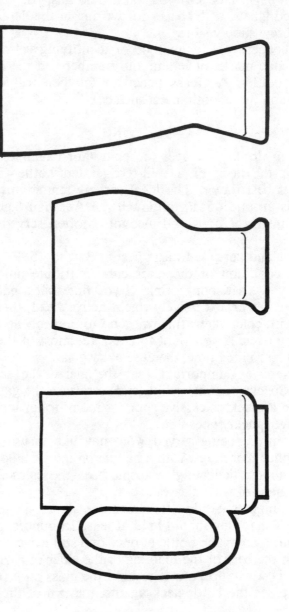

Beer Glasses

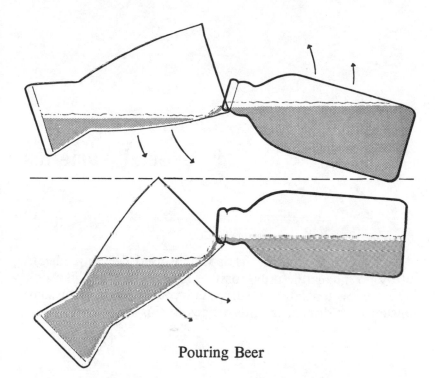

Pouring Beer

let the beverage run *gently* down the side of the glass. As the glass fills, turn it so that it becomes more upright. This produces an adequate, long-lasting head.

With practice you will learn to get the maximum amount of liquid from the bottle without pouring any slight yeast deposit that may be at the bottom.

PREPARING FOR COMPETITION

1. For competition purposes, do not use brown beer bottles, but present the beverage in a clear bottle so that the judges can see its color and clarity.

2. If there are no arrangements for chilling entries on the premises, keep your own bottles cold in an ice bucket until the moment when they must go on display. Then the judges will be able to taste your beverage at its chilly best.

3. If you hope to win any prizes, do not enter competition with beer, cider or perry that is less than three months old.

9. Special Varieties

Malt and hops are the most widely used beer ingredients, but by no means the only possible ones. If you feel like tickling your own palate, or surprising your friends, with some unusual long drinks, try the recipes in this chapter.

No. 25 GINGER BEER

❀

1 bottle ginger beer essence   1½ lb sugar
2½ gallons warm water   ½ packet baker's yeast

1. Mix sugar, water and essence.
2. When the mixture cools to 65°F. add yeast and stir thoroughly.
3. Bottle and cap at once. This will be ready to drink in two weeks.

No. 26 HONEY BEER

❖

I am indebted to my good friend James Hogg for this recipe. The end product is excellent!

5 lb honey	5 gallons water
2 lb corn sugar	1½ tsp acid blend
1 oz root ginger	Pure ale yeast starter
1 oz Kent hops	

1. Make the yeast starter three days in advance.

2. Boil the ginger, hops, sugar and honey in 2-1/2 gallons of water for half an hour. Stir occasionally to ensure thorough mixing and to avoid burning.

3. In the primary fermentor place the rest of the cold water, and stir in the acid blend. Then add the 2-1/2 gallons of hot mixture from the boiler.

4. When the wort cools to 70°F. add the yeast starter, and cover with sheet plastic, tied down.

5. Ferment at 55° to 65°F. till S.G. is between 1.005 and 1.010; then transfer to secondary fermentor and apply fermentation lock.

When fermentation is finished and the beer is perfectly clear, siphon it back into the primary fermentor, taking care not to disturb the sediment.

7. Add 1-1/2 cups corn sugar (no more!) and stir to dissolve.

8. Bottle in beer bottles, closed with crown caps.

9. Age 2-1/2 months.

No. 27 SPRUCE BEER

❄

Early settlers on this continent, who had no hops, used the green spring shoots of spruce trees to flavor their beer. This beer, by the way, also served as a remedy for scurvy. The spruce shoots provided some vitamin C, which was badly needed by people who had passed a long winter with no fresh vegetables.

You can try making it yourself with the spruce shoots if you wish, but I think you will find that the bottled spruce essence is more convenient – and besides, with the essence you can make spruce beer at any season of the year.

1 vial (2½ tbsp) spruce essence	1 tsp citric acid
1 lb pale malt extract	½ tsp yeast nutrient
1 lb sugar	Beer yeast starter
2½ gallons water	

(*N.B.:* The spruce essence is imported from England; most home-brew stores stock it, or will get it for you.)

1. Boil half the water with the sugar and malt extract for five minutes.

2. Pour into primary fermentor, adding citric acid, spruce essence, nutrient, and the rest of the cold water.

3. When the mixture has cooled to 65°F. add the yeast starter and cover.

4. When S.G. falls to 1.000 rack and bottle, adding 1/2 teaspoon sugar per bottle.

5. Seal with crown caps and age two to four weeks.

No. 28 ORANGE MEAD

❈

This recipe has one specially interesting feature: it will work out perfectly, even in the tropics, where the constant high temperatures are an obstacle to the production of other alcoholic beverages. If, in your home, you cannot find or make any cool corner for fermenting and aging the other recipes in this book, you can still produce orange mead.

2 lb honey
2 6-oz cans frozen orange juice
2 Campden tablets
1 tsp acid blend

¼ tsp grape tannin
½ tsp. Vita-Vin
1 gallon water
All-purpose or sherry yeast

Notes

1. Be sure that you use pure, fresh-frozen orange juice.
2. When the secondary fermentation has ceased, taste the mead. If it is completely dry (no residual sweetness) you can continue to feed it with sugar syrup, a little at a time, to obtain renewed fermentation and maximum alcohol content.
3. When fermentation is finally over you can, if you wish, add *a little* vermouth flavoring, to suit your taste.
4. This makes an interesting aperitif-style wine.

No. 29 BARLEY WINE

❈

This is a truly exceptional beverage, with all the flavor, aroma and sparkle of a fine ale, yet with an alcoholic content approaching that of a light wine.

8 lb Edme S.F.X. malt extract
5 gallons water
4 oz compressed hops *or* 8 oz hop extract
½ oz Kent finishing hops
2 lb corn sugar
1 tsp citric acid

1½ tsp salt
1 tsp brewing salts *or* ½ tsp yeast energizer
½ tsp gelatin finings
1 tsp ascorbic acid
1 oz gypsum
1 tsp heading liquid
Pure ale yeast starter

Starting gravity should be 1.060, terminal gravity 1.000. Process in the same way as ale but, because of the higher alcohol content, give it *plenty of time* to age in the bottle. I would advise at least two months, preferably much longer.

Acid blend – a mixture of organic acids (citric, tartaric and malic in equal parts) for correcting acid deficiency of musts.

Aerobic ferment – *see* Primary fermentation.

Aging – changes occurring in a fermented beverage, after fermentation is finished, which improve its flavor.

Alcohol – ethyl alcohol, C_2H_5OH, the preservative and intoxicating ingredient of fermented beverages. Roughly half the weight of sugar in the original ingredients is converted to alcohol.

Ale – beverage similar to beer, but containing more alcohol.

Anaerobic ferment – *see* Secondary fermentation.

Antioxidant – a substance added to a beverage, usually just before bottling, to prevent excess oxidation. Ascorbic acid and sodium erythorbate are good antioxidants.

Autolysis – consumption of yeast sediment by live yeast; can produce bad flavors unless prevented by timely racking.

Balling scale – hydrometer scale indicating sugar content of wort or must in percentage by weight.

Barley – cereal grain commonly used as the basic ingredient of beer.

Baster – small glass or plastic syringe, useful for taking samples of liquids.

Beer – a low-alcohol fermented beverage, usually flavored with hops.

Boiler – container for boiling the mash in beermaking.

Brewing hops – strong-flavored hops used during the boiling of the wort.

Brewing salts – a nutrient additive that helps the fermentation of beer yeast.

Brix scale – same as Balling scale.

Campden tablets – 7-grain tablets of potassium metabisulphite. Dissolved in fruit juices or similar acid solutions, they release sulphur dioxide which acts as a sterilant and antioxidant. Not recommended for use with beer.

Capping machine – a hand-operated machine to put crown caps on beer or soft-drink bottles. Essential for beermaking.

Carbon dioxide – CO_2, the gas given off by fermenting yeast. Roughly half the weight of sugar is given off as CO_2.

Carboy – narrow-necked glass or plastic vessel, 4 to 15 gallons capacity, used with fermentation lock as secondary fermentor.

Cellulose fiber – used in pressing fruit to increase the output of juice.

Chlorine detergent – a powerful sterilant for cleaning bottles and equipment. It kills wine and beer yeast, so it must be rinsed off after use.

Cider – fermented apple juice, usually containing not more than 8% alcohol. May be still or sparkling, sweet or dry.

Cider base – a compound of sugar and fruit acids that can replace fresh apple juice in cidermaking.

Concentrate – strained, dehydrated fruit extract, much used instead of fresh fruit for making cider and perry.

Crusher – a mechanical device for breaking up apples and pears prior to pressing.

Cyser – a beverage made of apple juice and honey, stronger than cider.

Dry – a beverage is said to be dry when it contains less than 1% residual unfermented sugar.

Energizer – nutrient added to increase efficiency of yeast. Usually contains phosphates plus vitamin B.

Enzyme – additive used to economize ingredients and speed production in beermaking and winemaking.

Fermentation lock – low-pressure valve of glass or plastic; permits escape of CO_2 from secondary fermentor, but excludes air and bacteria.

Finishing hops – hops added to beer after the wort has been boiled, to lend aroma to the beer.

Floculation – coalescence and settling of yeast cells to a firm deposit.

Gallon – Canadian or imperial gallon = 160 imp. fluid ounces. U.S. or reputed gallon = 128 U.S. fluid ounces. Check recipes and container sizes to avoid errors.

Head – the layer of foam on beer when poured into a glass.

Heading agent – additive that produces a thick, long-lasting head on beer.

110

Hydrometer – instrument for measuring density of a liquid. Essential for sugar control and other purposes in home-brewing.

Hydrometer testing jar – glass or plastic cylinder in which to float the hydrometer.

Keeving – settling process that removes solids from apple or pear juice before fermentation.

Lager – a light beer, yellow in color.

Lees – yeast sediment in bottom of fermentation vessel.

Malt – a barley product which provides sugar, and much of the flavor and color, in beermaking.

Malt extract – generally used instead of malt by home-brewers.

Mash – the mixture of ingredients that is brewed for beermaking.

Mead – a beverage whose main fermentable ingredient is honey.

Metabisulphite – sodium or potassium metabisulphite, used to provide sulphur dioxide as a sterilant or antioxidant. Not recommended for use with beer.

Must – crushed fruit, juice and other ingredients prior to fermentation for cider or perry.

Mycoderma – spoilage organism that consumes alcohol and impairs flavor of fermented beverages.

Nutrient – nitrogen-producing salts added to invigorate yeast and produce more alcohol and clearer beverages.

Oxidation – an unwelcome chemical reaction with oxygen, which impairs the flavor and color of fermented beverages.

Pectic enzyme – enzyme that breaks down pectin in fruit, releasing more juice, color and flavor.

Pectin – a constituent of some fruits which tends to cause cloudiness in cider and perry. Eliminated by use of pectic enzyme.

Perry – fermented pear juice, usually containing not more than 8% alcohol. May be still or sparkling, sweet or dry.

Porter – a rich, dark-brown alcoholic beverage, containing 4% to 6% alcohol.

Potential alcohol – an estimate, based on sugar content of the ingredients, of the percentage of alcohol that will be achieved in the finished beverage.

Press – machine for forcing juice out of fruit pulp.

Primary fermentation – first stage of fermentation in which most yeast growth takes place, and in which air is sometimes allowed to reach the ingredients.

Primary fermentor – open-topped vessel in which primary fermentation takes place.

Proof – a 100-degree scale for measurement of alcoholic strength of beverages, with different meanings in different countries. In Canada and Britain 100 proof = 57.1% alcohol by volume, so 70 proof is about 40% alcohol by volume. In the United States 100 proof = 50% alcohol by volume. To avoid misunderstandings, this book describes alcoholic strength only in percentage by volume.

Racking – siphoning a beverage from one vessel to another, so as to leave behind the lees or sediment.

Secondary fermentation – a fermentation from which air is excluded, sometimes called anaerobic fermentation. Most of the alcohol is produced during this stage.

Secondary fermentor – carboy or other narrow-necked vessel, fitted with a fermentation lock.

Sparkling beverage – beverage containing CO_2; effervesces when bottle is opened. All beers are sparkling.

Specific gravity – S.G., the ratio between the density of a substance and the density of water. Unfermented worts and musts have S.G. higher than 1.000. Finished beers usually have S.G. of about 1.000.

Stabilizer – sorbic acid, a non-toxic, tasteless chemical added to prevent renewed fermentation of a beverage in bottle. It will not stop active fermentation.

Starter – a strongly fermenting yeast culture used to start fermentation in a larger volume of wort or must.

Sterilants – chemicals used to inhibit wild yeasts and spoilage bacteria in brewing ingredients or on equipment.

Stout – a heavy, dark-brown or black beverage containing more alcohol than beer.

Sulphur dioxide – SO_2, the gas released by Campden tablets and metabisulphites; a useful sterilant and antioxidant for certain home-brewing purposes, but not for use with beer.

Sweet – a fermented beverage containing 1% or more residual sugar after fermentation is finished.

Water treatment – an additive used when water is too soft to make good beer.

Yeast – microscopic fungus which consumes sugar, producing alcohol and carbon dioxide. Cultured yeasts make the best fermented beverages.

TABLES AND CONVERSION FORMULAS

Fluid-measure Equivalents

Note that although the United States and Canadian (imperial) fluid measures have the same names – fluid ounce, pint, quart and gallon – they differ considerably in capacity. When using recipes from other books and magazines, be sure you know which system of units the author is using.

1 imperial gallon = 160 imperial fluid ounces = 4.5459 liters = 1.2 U.S. gallons

1 U.S. gallon = 128 U.S. fluid ounces = 3.7853 liters = 0.833 imperial gallon

5 imperial gallons = 6 U.S. gallons

1 imperial gallon of pure water weighs 10 pounds

1 U.S. gallon of pure water weighs 8 pounds 5.3 ounces

1 U.S. pint = 16 U.S. fluid ounces

1 imperial pint = 20 imperial fluid ounces

1 U.S. fluid ounce = 1.805 cubic inches = 1.041 imperial fluid ounces

1 imperial fluid ounce = 1.734 cubic inches = 0.961 U.S. fluid ounces

1 cup = 8 U.S. fluid ounces = 0.5 U.S. pint = .417 imperial pint

Weight-measure Equivalents

United States and Canadian (imperial) weight measures are identical.

1 pound = 16 ounces = 453.592 grams = .45359 kilogram

1 kilogram = 1000 grams = 35.274 ounces = 2.2046 pounds

1 ounce = 28.35 grams

Temperature Equivalents

a) To convert Fahrenheit to Centigrade

$$F.° - 32 \div 1.8 = C.°$$

Example: To convert 68°F. to Centigrade

$$68 - 32 = 36$$
$$36 \div 1.8 = 20$$
$$68°F. = 20°C.$$

b) To convert Centigrade to Fahrenheit

$$C.° \times 1.8 + 32 = F.°$$

Example: To convert 15°C. to Fahrenheit

$$15 \times 1.8 = 27$$
$$27 + 32 = 59$$
$$15°C. = 59°F.$$

Hydrometer Correction Table

A hydrometer is designed to read at one temperature. If the must is above or below that temperature the reading will be inaccurate. The following table is for a hydrometer whose standard temperature is 59°F.

Temperature of liquid	Correction
50°F.	Subtract .0006
59°F.	None
68°F.	Add .0009
77°F.	Add .002
86°F.	Add .0034
95°F.	Add .005
104°F.	Add .0068

Example: If the temperature of the must is 95°F. and the hydrometer gives a specific gravity reading of 1.105, add .005. The correct S.G. will then be 1.110.

114

Corrections for temperatures falling between those shown in the table are worked out arithmetically. For example, take a temperature of 98°F. The 9 degrees between 95° and 104° in the table result in a difference of .0018 in the correction column (.0068 – .005). The 3 degrees between 95° and 98° will therefore give a correction of one-third of .0018, or .0006. As the hydrometer reads to 3 decimal places, this means that you add .001 to the reading.

Proof Conversion Table

Note that "proof" is an arbitrary level of alcoholic strength, differing from one country to another. This table shows the percentage equivalents of three commonly used proof scales.

% Absolute Alcohol by volume	Canadian Proof rating	Degrees of Proof, Sykes Scale	Equivalent U.S. Proof rating
100	75 Over Proof	175	200
97	70 O.P.	170	194
94	65 O.P.	165	188
91	60 O.P.	160	182
86	50 O.P.	150	172
80	40 O.P.	140	160
74	30 O.P.	130	148
69	20 O.P.	120	138
63	10 O.P.	110	126
57.1	Proof	100	114.2
51	10 Under Proof	90	102
46	20 U.P.	80	92
42.5	25 U.P.	75	85
40	30 U.P.	70	80
34	40 U.P.	60	68
29	50 U.P.	50	58
23	60 U.P.	40	46
17	70 U.P.	30	34
11	80 U.P.	20	22
6	90 U.P.	10	12
0	100 U.P.	0	0

Conversion Table: Specific Gravity at 60°F. to Balling
Assuming S.G. of water at 60°F. is unity.

Degrees Balling	Specific Gravity	Degrees Balling	Specific Gravity
0.00	1.000	15.0	1.059
0.50	1.002	15.5	1.062
1.00	1.004	16.0	1.064
1.50	1.006	16.5	1.066
2.00	1.008	17.0	1.068
2.50	1.010	17.5	1.070
3.00	1.012	18.0	1.072
3.50	1.014	18.5	1.075
4.00	1.016	19.0	1.077
4.50	1.017	19.5	1.079
5.00	1.019	20.0	1.081
5.50	1.021	20.5	1.084
6.00	1.023	21.0	1.086
6.50	1.025	21.5	1.088
7.00	1.027	22.0	1.090
7.50	1.029	22.5	1.093
8.00	1.031	23.0	1.095
8.50	1.033	23.5	1.097
9.00	1.035	24.0	1.099
9.50	1.037	24.5	1.102
10.0	1.039	25.0	1.104
10.5	1.041	25.5	1.106
11.0	1.043	26.0	1.109
11.5	1.045	26.5	1.111
12.0	1.048	27.0	1.113
12.5	1.050	27.5	1.116
13.0	1.052	28.0	1.118
13.5	1.054	28.5	1.120
14.0	1.056	29.0	1.123
14.5	1.058	29.5	1.125
		30.0	1.127

Specific Gravity – Potential Alcohol Table

This table shows the alcohol yield you may expect in relation to the specific gravity of the wort or must.

Specific Gravity	Potential alcohol % by volume	Specific Gravity	Potential alcohol % by volume
1.000	0	1.070	9.2
1.005	0.5	1.075	9.9
1.010	0.9	1.080	10.6
1.015	1.6	1.085	11.3
1.020	2.3	1.090	12.0
1.025	3.0	1.095	12.7
1.030	3.7	1.100	13.4
1.035	4.4	1.105	14.1
1.040	5.1	1.110	14.9
1.045	5.8	1.115	15.6
1.050	6.5	1.120	16.3
1.055	7.2	1.125	17.0
1.060	7.8	1.130	17.7
1.065	8.6	1.135	18.4

Note: Some published conversion tables show higher yields of alcohol than does this. But most home-made beverages do not contain as much alcohol as such tables suggest, and as some home-brewers seem to expect.

There is a serious disadvantage in overestimating the strength of your beverages, because they are less stable and more subject to contamination than you think they are. You are far better off to have .5% more alcohol than you had expected.

STANLEY ANDERSON is the operator of the Wine-Art chain of stores that supplies directions, materials, and equipment for making wine and beer at home. Mr. Anderson is the publisher of a magazine for the oenologist and lives in Vancouver.

RAYMOND HULL, an enormously productive freelance author, also lives in Vancouver and is currently working on a half-dozen books as he writes magazine articles, plays, and TV scripts, and organizes his own educational TV program.